the
BEST
of
California's Riviera

recipes from the most popular

restaurants of

the Gold Coast of California

ISBN 0-9627302-3-8
First Edition
May, 1993
The Newport Press
Newport Beach, CA

CREDITS

Publisher:

The Newport Press
Box 3477, Suite 161
Newport Beach, CA 92663
(714) 645-7540

Editors:

Ron Garrison, Publisher and Editor-in-Chief
Sue Jeffries, Home Economist
Mary Lou Kiley

Photography:

Cover and dessert photographs courtesy of John Dominis Restaurant, Newport Beach, CA

Remaining photography courtesy of Pavilion, Four Seasons Hotel, Newport Beach, CA

Printer:

Orange County Lithograph Co.
Anaheim, CA

PREFACE

Some four years ago, The Newport Press embarked on a project to create a book similar to this one. However, it was much narrower in scope, as "the Best of Newport" focused solely on the restaurants of Newport Beach. Although the book proved highly successful, it was quickly evident that to focus solely on a singular city is not only too narrow in defining the experience of California's Riviera but also a disservice to the surrounding cities. They too, are equally important to the vitality of the region. To define the "Riviera" as only miles of coastline is an injustice to the total experience and enjoyment of living or vacationing in the area. Therefore, the concept of "the Best of California's Riviera" was born.

Our goal was to design and create a book that reflected a true cross section of the dining experience in this area. We believe we have accomplished that. We began in Newport, reaching south through Corona del Mar, Laguna Beach and Dana Point. To the east, Costa Mesa, Santa Ana and Irvine were embraced.

The coast of Southern California has long been special to all who visit or live here. Whether one stops by for a frozen banana, dines at one of the elegant restaurants overlooking the beautiful harbors or has dinner steps away from the Orange County Performing Arts Center, a lasting memory assuredly will be etched with a grateful and satisfying smile. Thus, it is appropriate to recognize these wonderful restaurants who bring us an exciting variety of cuisines.

The staff of "the Best of California's Riviera" wishes to extend their gratitude to the owners, managers and the chefs of the participating restaurants. Without their cooperation this book would not have been possible. We thank the general public, for without their loyal patronage, these restaurants would not have remained so popular.

It should be pointed out that some of the enclosed recipes are not necessarily served on a daily basis. They are possibly "specials" or may be limited, due to the seasonality of major ingredients. Therefore, we highly recommend that prospective chefs enjoy a given dish at its respective restaurant prior to preparing it at home.

Enjoy and Bon Appetit!

TABLE of CONTENTS

RESTAURANTS IN ALPHABETICAL ORDER

Blue Beet Cafe

Critique, Blue Beet's Caesar Salad (Salads & Dressings, pg. 57)
Beef Stroganoff (Entrees Meat, pg. 83)
Bay Scallops, Gina Marie (Entrees Seafood, pg. 139)
Raspberry Delight (Desserts, pg. 196)
Shooting Star (Potpourri, pg. 213)
Tortuga (Potpourri, pg. 214)

Cafe 5-0-5

Critique, Chicken Fiesta Salad (Salads & Dressings, pg. 63)

Cafe Lido

Critique, New Zealand Cockle Clams (Appetizers, pg. 24)
Oysters Felix (Appetizers, pg. 24)

The Cannery

Critique, Chicken Champignon (Entrees Poultry, pg. 115)
Orange Roughy with Lemon Caper Butter (Entrees Seafood, pg. 154)
Seafood Tacos (Entrees Seafood, pg. 158)

Cano's

Critique, Dungeness Crab Cakes with Dijon Mustard and Lime Sauce (Entrees Seafood,
   pg. 146)

Carmelo's Ristorante Italiano & Continentale

Critique, Saltimbocca alla Romana (Entrees Meat, pg. 101)
Agnolotti alla Panna (Entrees Pasta, pg. 167)

Ciao Mein

Critique, Mongolian Beef (Entrees Meat, pg. 95)
Papardelle (Entrees Pasta, pg. 174)

The Chart House

Critique, Chart House Bleu Cheese Dressing (Salads & Dressings, pg. 62)
Chart House Mud Pie (Desserts, pg. 185)

Claes'

Critique, Garvad Lax (Appetizers, pg. 17)
Pacific Oyster Stew (Soup, pg. 43)
Claes' Salad Dressing (Salads & Dressings, pg. 63)
Monkfish with Caramelized Shallot Sauce (Entrees Seafood, pg. 153)
Grapefruit-Tarragon Sorbet (Desserts, pg. 193)
Mango Sorbet (Desserts, pg. 193)

Oysters

Critique, Baked Brie in Pastry (Appetizers, pg. 3)
Oyster Stew (Soups, pg. 42)
Baked Salmon in Phyllo with Orange-Ginger Sauce (Entrees Seafood, pg. 138)

The Palm Garden

Critique, Mesquite Grilled Chicken Breast, Stuffed with Goat Cheese and Sun Dried
    Tomatoes with Roasted Garlic Rosemary Butter (Entrees Poultry, pg. 119)
Raspberry, Strawberry and Blueberry Sabayon Parfait (Desserts, pg. 197)
Mexican and Thai Shrimp Pizza (Potpourri, pg. 211)

Paradise Cafe

Critique, Chicken Moutard (Entrees Poultry, pg. 117)
Paradise Pan Roast (Entrees Seafood, pg. 154)

Park Avenue Cafe

Critique, Chicken Cordon Bleu (Entrees Poultry, pg. 114)

Pavilion

Critique, Grilled Scallops with Truffle Lobster Potatoes (Appetizers, pg. 18)
Lobster and Frog Legs Wrapped in Phyllo (Appetizers, pg. 21)
Lightly Spiced Corn Chowder with House Smoked Shrimp (Soups, pg. 40)
Tomato, Avocado and Maui Onion Salad (Salads & Dressings, pg. 75)
Black Angus Striploin with a Four Peppercorn Crust (Entrees Meat, pg. 84)
Black Angus Tenderloin with a Bone Marrow and Aromatic Herb Crust (Entrees Meat,
    pg. 84)
Boneless Rack of Colorado Lamb with Pepper Herb Crust and Chive Mashed Potatoes
    (Entrees Meat, pg. 85)
Loin of Rabbit with Braised White Cabbage and Madeira Sauce (Entrees Meat, pg. 92)
Grilled Ahi with a Balsamic Herb Sauce (Entrees Seafood, pg. 147)
"Pavilion" Zucchini Walnut Bread (Desserts, pg. 195)
Raspberry and Lemon Cream Napoleon (Desserts, pg. 196)

The Quiet Woman

Critique, Marinated Pork Chops (Entrees Meat, pg. 93)
New York Pepper Steak (Entrees Meat, pg. 97)
Chicken Teriyaki (Entrees Poultry, pg. 128)
Swordfish Pasta (Entrees Pasta, pg. 178)
Toll House Pie (Desserts, pg. 198)
Butternut Squash (Potpourri, pg. 204)

Tutto Mare

Villa Nova

The Warehouse

Watercolors

The Wine Cellar

Woody's Wharf

APPETIZERS

APPETIZERS

OYSTERS

2515 E. Coast Hwy.
Corona del Mar, CA
675-7411

The overall feeling of Oysters is very upbeat California from the color scheme of aqua and white to the background music which is soft jazz. Guests may enjoy dining in the Main Room with comfortable booths, the glass enclosed Garden Room or the Outdoor Patio for streetside cafe style dining. Oysters offers a refreshing menu of red oak grilled fish, steaks, poultry and tempting pasta dishes. An extensive wine list and a beautiful oak wood bar compliment the Oyster Bar menu where chefs create delightful appetizers, pastas and their many signature oyster dishes. Oysters is open daily for lunch and dinner and serves brunch on Sunday. Live jazz is offered on Friday and Saturday evenings.

Baked Brie in Pastry

2	5" x 5" French puff pastry squares, 1/4" thick
2	3" x 3" squares 60% brie cheese
2	teaspoons jalapeno preserves
2	teaspoons red currant jelly
1/4	cup chopped hazel nuts
2	eggs
2	teaspoons water
	flour, just enough to cover pastry board

Place flour on cutting board. Roll out pastry until it is an 8 inch by 8 inch square. Cut two lines across the tops of the cheese squares. In the first cut, place jalapeno preserves. In the second cut, place the red currant jelly. Top each with the hazel nuts. Invert the cheese onto the pastry squares. Fold pastry over the corners of the cheese after brushing with egg wash (2 eggs and 2 teaspoons of water, mixed thoroughly). Turn over the pastry and brush the tops of the pastry. Bake in a preheated oven at 400 degrees on an oiled pie pan for 20-25 minutes until golden brown. Serve with fresh fruit, berries and thin slices of Baguette bread. Serves four.

FISHERMAN'S RESTAURANT AND BAR

1 McFadden Pl.
Newport Pier
Newport Beach, CA
675-9771

Fisherman's has perhaps the most unique location of all the restaurants in Newport Beach, namely at the end of the Newport Pier. Along with a great view of the Pacific Ocean and with Catalina Island on the horizon, diners can enjoy a variety of seafood, steaks and poultry. Upstairs, you will find an oyster bar and an outdoor patio for dining or enjoying your favorite libation. Fisherman's is open daily for lunch and dinner.

Baked Oysters

6	*halved oysters*
2	*ounces parmesan cheese*
2	*slices bacon, cooked crisply*
1	*green onion, finely chopped*

Sprinkle parmesan cheese over oysters and bake at 300 degrees until cheese is melted and slightly browned. Remove from the oven, sprinkle with chopped onion and bacon bits. Serves one.

FIVES CROWNS

3801 E. Coast Hwy.
Corona del Mar, CA
760-0331

Upon entering Corona del Mar from the south, one of the first notable sites is of a charming English country inn named Five Crowns, now serving the community for over 25 years. Their apparent secret for success is a regard for food rather than a latest fad. The menu ranges from their classic prime rib to new innovative dishes of the California cuisine. Five Crowns' extensive wine list (over 1200 labels) has earned numerous awards. In fact, if anything is lacking at Five Crowns, it is the lack of wall space for all the awards this establishment has earned. Dinner is served daily along with brunch on Sundays.

Broiled Oysters with Shallots and Balsamic Vinegar

16	*fresh oysters*
16	*basil leaves*
	freshly ground black pepper, to taste
	rock salt
1/4	*cup balsamic vinegar*
3	*tablespoons chopped shallots*

Open oysters and discard flat half of the shell. Detach the meat completely and place a basil leaf underneath it on the remaining half of the shell. Season with black pepper. In an ovenproof dish, place a thin layer of rock salt (to minimize tipping) and arrange the oysters on top. Place the dish in a preheated broiler 5 inches from the heat for 3 to 4 minutes, or until the oysters begin to "curl". Remove, top with vinegar and shallots and serve warm. Serves four.

RUMPELSTILTSKIN'S

114 McFadden Pl.
Newport Beach, CA
673-5025

Located in the heart of Old Newport at the Newport Pier, Rumples (as the locals call it) is well known for its live entertainment and dancing. However, Rumples' kitchen is not to be outdone. Its Scampi Alfredo (the house specialty) is renowned among the local residents. Dinner is best enjoyed in the early evening before the bar crowd arrives. Rumples offers a fun, casual evening of dining and dancing for those so inclined. And for the romantic at heart, a quiet walk along the shore of the Pacific Ocean beckons right out the front door.

Buffalo Wings

2	pounds chicken wings, tips discarded
4	cups safflower oil
1	tablespoon minced garlic
1/2	cup minced onion
1/2	jalapeno pepper, seeded and minced
1/4	cup green pepper, minced
2	tablespoons Italian parsley, chopped
1	tablespoon bacon drippings
1	cup ketchup
1/2	cup cider vinegar
2	tablespoons sugar
2	tablespoons tabasco Sauce
1	tablespoon worcestershire sauce
1/2	teaspoon liquid smoke
1/2	teaspoon black pepper
1/4	teaspoon dried oregano
1/4	teaspoon crushed red pepper
1/4	teaspoon dried sweet basil

Saute garlic, onion, jalapeno, green pepper and parsley in bacon drippings until onion is soft. Add all remaining ingredients except the oil and chicken wings. Bring to a boil and simmer over low heat for 15 minutes. Bring oil to 350 degrees and deep fry the wings in small batches for 5 minutes. Drain and place wings in an ovenproof dish. Cover with the sauce and bake for 15 minutes at 350 degrees. Serve with blue cheese dressing and plenty of napkins.

ANTONELLO RISTORANTE

South Coast Plaza Village
1611 Sunflower Ave.
Santa Ana, CA
751-7153

Since 1979, Antonello Ristorante has been taking diners on a journey to the Old World with its extensive menu of extraordinary Italian cuisine and vast wine list. Set amid a warm, romantic and luxurious atmosphere, Antonello has been frequented by foreign dignitaries, celebrities and others who demand the highest quality dining experience. This critically acclaimed restaurant features a wide variety of Italian dishes. Carlito Jocson, the executive chef has brought together an innovative and lighter cuisine that has produced numerous awards for the restaurant and himself. Here are three variations of Antonello's favorite carpaccios.

Carpaccio ai Pini e Olive

1	8 ounce beef filet, sliced paper thin
1	tablespoon calamata nuts, chopped
1	tablespoon pine nuts
	parmesan cheese to taste
	extra virgin olive oil, enough to cover the filet slices
	squeeze of fresh lemon juice
	ground black pepper to taste

Cover a serving plate with the meat slices. Add the remaining ingredients. Serves two to four.

Carpaccio con Rughetta

1	8 ounce beef filet, sliced paper thin
1/4	cup arugola, cut julienne
	extra virgin olive oil, enough to cover the meat slices
	squeeze of fresh lemon juice
	ground black pepper to taste

Cover a serving plate with the meat slices and add the remaining ingredients. Serves two to four.

Carpaccio Italiano

1   8 ounce beef filet, sliced paper thin
2   teaspoons capers
1/8   cup shaved parmesan cheese
        extra virgin olive oil, enough to cover the meat slices
        squeeze of fresh lemon juice
        ground black pepper to taste

Cover a serving plate with the meat slices. Add the remaining ingredients and serve. Serves two to four.

VILLA NOVA
3131 W. Coast Hwy.
Newport Beach, CA
642-7880

To the tourists and locals alike the restaurant, Villa Nova, needs no introduction. This landmark restaurant with its unique exterior, a massive mural of rural Italy has long been a favorite of all who enjoy the best Italian cuisine. Located on Pacific Coast Highway and overlooking the beautiful Newport Harbor, Villa Nova offers an extensive menu and wine list. Those seeking the finest in Italian dining will find it here. Entertainment is offered most weekends.

Carpaccio con Grana

1   6 ounce filet mignon
1   teaspoon extra virgin olive oil
1   tablespoon grated grana parmesan
3/4   tablespoon capers

Place the filet in a freezer until firm, not frozen. Slice 3 to 5 paper thin slices and place on a serving plate. Sprinkle with the capers and grana. Add the olive oil. Serves one.

TUTTO MARE

545 Fashion Island
Newport Beach, CA
640-6333

Loosely translated in Italian, Tutto Mare means "Everything from the Sea". Tutto Mare chefs appear to offer everything, specializing in foods from the coastal regions of Italy. The menu includes whole fresh fish baked in an oak-burning oven, homemade pastas, charcoal grilled and spit roasted meat, fowl and fresh fish. Tutto Mare is open Monday through Saturday for lunch. Dinner is served daily.

Carpaccio de Salmone
(Raw Grappa Cured Salmon Slices)

1   raw boned side of salmon, sliced with skin on

Marinade:

       Grappa (Italian brandy) enough to cover slices
       equal parts of sugar and salt to cover
       one bunch whole dillweed, chopped
1   tablespoon pink peppercorns

Cover fish with marinade and refrigerate for 6 hours or more. Remove from marinade and serve as an appetizer with bread rounds.

ROYAL KHYBER
1000 N. Bristol St.
Newport Beach, CA
752-5200

Royal Khyber is the first Indian restaurant to ever serve Orange County. For over 12 years, this outstanding restaurant has been serving authentic Tandoori cuisine elegantly presented in the Moghul tradition. Owner Arun Puri insists that only the freshest foods are used and only naturally grown spices flavor their dishes. They do not use lard, animal fat, eggs, cream, flour or MSG in their sauces. In this day of heightened health consciousness, it is refreshing not to be concerned while dining at the Royal Khyber. With the decor of palatial comfort and secluded tables, one can truly enjoy the cuisine of the East. Belly dancing is offered every Friday and Saturday night.

Chicken Tikka

Marinade:

1/4	cup yogurt
2 1/2	tablespoons ginger paste
2 1/2	tablespoons garlic paste
1/2	teaspoon white pepper
1/2	teaspoon cumin powder
1/3	teaspoon mace
1/3	teaspoon nutmeg
1/3	teaspoon green cardamom powder
1/2	teaspoon red chili powder
1/2	teaspoon turmeric
4	tablespoons fresh lemon juice
2	tablespoons flour
1/2	teaspoon salt
5	tablespoons vegetable oil

1 3/4   pounds chicken legs, skinned, boned and each leg cut into 4 pieces
1/4   cup melted butter

In a medium bowl, combine all the ingredients except for the chicken and butter. Mix well so that they are well blended. Rub the chicken in the mixture and let marinate for 4 hours. Divide the chicken into 6 parts. Put the chicken on 6 skewers and grill for 6 to 7 minutes. Turn often to insure evenness in cooking. Baste the chicken with melted butter while grilling. Serves four.

JOSH SLOCUM'S

2601 W. Coast Hwy.
Newport Beach, CA
642-5935

Josh Slocum was the first man to sail around the world singlehanded in the 1890's. This restaurant named for him, is located overlooking the Newport Harbor. Offering a variety of fresh fish, steaks and poultry, one can enjoy a pleasant evening of dining while enjoying the beautiful yachts sailing by. Josh Slocum's is open daily for dinner. The attire is casual.

Chilled Stuffed Artichoke

1   *artichoke, boiled until tender (30-45 minutes)*

Stuffing:

1/2   *cup mayonnaise*
3   *tablespoons dijon mustard*
         pinch of tarragon leaves
1/4   *cup bay shrimp*

Combine all ingredients and chill for 1/2 hour. Pull out the center leaves and clean the heart of the artichoke. Fill the center with the stuffing and serve with a lemon wedge.

EL TORITO GRILL

59 Fashion Island
Newport Beach, CA
640-2875

To enter the El Torito Grill excites one immediately. Its festive decor and cheery atmosphere along with the odors emitting from the kitchen definitely whets one's appetite. The menu offers a broad variety of Nuevo-Mexican dishes along with traditional fare that always has a unique twist to it. For a different and delightful dining experience be sure to try the Sunday Brunch. It is unlike any brunch you may have experienced in the past.

Blue Corn Nachos

24   *large blue corn tortilla chips*
1   *cup black beans (see below)*
1/4   *cups shredded jack cheese*
2   *tablespoons cilantro, chopped*
1/2   *cup shredded lettuce (may be half cabbage, if desired)*
1/2   *cup sour cream*
1   *cup guacamole*
1/2   *cup pico de gallo (see below)*

Preheat broiler. Selecting large, flat blue corn chips, spread each chip with black beans, sprinkle generously with shredded cheese, place chips on cookie sheet and broil for 1 minute or until cheese is melted. Remove and place on large serving platter, sprinkling with chopped cilantro. In middle of plate, place lettuce mix, top with sour cream and guacamole side by side, spoon pico de gallo between sour cream and guacamole, and garnish with fresh cilantro sprigs. Serve immediately.

Optional: After spreading chips with beans and cheese, top each chip with a small amount of diced, grilled chicken or steak.

Black beans:

1   *cup dried black beans*
1   *small yellow onion, chopped*
1   *garlic clove, minced*
3   *cups water*
        salt to taste
        ground black pepper to taste

Check beans for any stones. Combine all ingredients except salt and pepper in a large saucepan over high heat. Bring to a boil. Reduce heat and simmer uncovered for 1/2 hours, or until beans are tender. Add salt and pepper to taste. Remove from heat and cool slightly. Place beans in a food processor or blender, and mash carefully, making sure beans maintain some chunky texture. If beans have too much liquid, place in a skillet and cook until liquid has evaporated.

Pico de gallo:

3	medium tomatoes, diced
1/4	red onion, diced fine
1/4	yellow onion, diced fine
2	serrano chilies, seeded and diced fine
1/4	bunch cilantro, coarsely chopped
	juice of 1/2 lime or more to taste
	salt to taste
1	garlic clove, minced
1/4	teaspoon dried oregano

Place chopped ingredients into a mixing container. Add lime juice and seasonings; mix well but gently. Keep refrigerated until ready for use. Serves six.

MAXI'S GRILLE

Red Lion Inn, Orange County Airport
3050 Bristol Street
Costa Mesa, CA
540-7000

Maxi's Grille offers a truly unique and eclectic menu. Such items as Alligator and Calamari Salad or the Georgia Peanut Salad (See Salad section) are just a couple of the interesting items to whet your appetite. Entrees include pasta, fresh fish, steaks, game, rack of lamb and free range chicken and veal. Executive Chef Jonathan Litvack's philosophy of freshness, health, quality, variety and price-value is strictly enforced. Maxi's even has its own garden on the premises to ensure only the freshest of herbs and spices are used. Dinner is served daily.

Escargot

24	large escargot
1/4	cup pancetta bacon
1/4	cup wild mushrooms, sliced
1	tablespoon dijon mustard
1	cup heavy cream
1/4	cup finely diced onion
4	each brioche

Saute the bacon and onion in a saute pan. Add mushrooms and escargot. Continue to cook until escargot is warmed through. Add the mustard and cream and reduce until lightly thickened. Cut off the tops of the brioche and place 6 escargot in each with a little sauce over the top. Set top to the side of the dish and garnish with a sprig of tarragon. Serves four.

ANTONELLO RISTORANTE

South Coast Plaza Village
1611 Sunflower Ave.
Santa Ana, CA
751-7153

Fagioli e Gamberi
(Beans and Shrimp)

1	*cup cannelini beans, canned and cooked (Italian brand preferred)*
1/2	*pound bay shrimp, cooked*
1	*tablespoon balsamic vinegar*
1/4	*cup extra virgin olive oil*
1	*tablespoon finely chopped Italian parsley*

Boil salted water in 2 quart pot. Place the beans and shrimp in a strainer and submerge into the boiling water and blanch for 1 minute. Lift the strainer and drain until the beans and shrimp are dry. Place the beans and shrimp in a mixing bowl, toss with olive oil, balsamic vinegar and parsley. Salt and pepper to taste and serve immediately. Serves two.

THE WAREHOUSE

3450 Via Oporto
Newport Beach, CA
673-4700

Located on the waterfront of Newport Harbor in Lido Village, this restaurant has the unique distinction of being dedicated to the legendary actor, John Wayne, who lived in Newport Beach. The fare is as one might suspect, heavily weighted towards fresh seafood. However, Chef Charles, a noted California chef, always gives the fare a delicious twist. The Warehouse offers dining on its heated patio or one may dine upstairs overlooking the harbor. Live entertainment is offered on weekends. On Sundays, brunch is offered on the heated patio. The Warehouse is open daily for lunch and dinner.

Garlic Shrimp

4	*3 1/2 ounce ramekins*
16	*shrimp (21/25 count), peeled, veined, and cooked*
4	*bread rounds*

Garlic Butter:

1/4	*pound sweet butter*
2	*tablespoons parsley, chopped*
2	*garlic cloves, minced*
	salt and pepper to taste

Beat butter until smooth and mix with rest of ingredients. Refrigerate until needed.

Tomato Caulis:

1	*ounce sweet butter*
2	*tomatoes, peeled, seeded, and chopped*
2	*tablespoons shallots, finely chopped*

Melt butter in a saucepan, saute shallots (do not brown). Add tomatoes and reduce until the liquid has evaporated. Season with salt and pepper.

Bread rounds:

Cut bread into rounds with a cookie cutter, slightly smaller than the ramekins in diameter. Lightly spread one side with garlic butter. Spoon 1 tablespoon tomato caulis into

each ramekin. Place 4 shrimp into each ramekin, cover with 1 tablespoon garlic butter and top with a bread round, buttered side up. Bake in oven until bread is lightly browned.

CLAES'

Hotel Laguna
425 S. Coast Hwy.
Laguna Beach, CA
494-1151

Claes' located at the historic Hotel Laguna, offers an oceanview dining experience that very few can match. Owner Claes Andersen has brought Chef Todd Clore to the restaurant. Reflecting his passion and commitment to perfection, Chef Clore has created and designed an innovative menu that yet maintains the traditional and historic values Hotel Laguna has offered over the many years. Equally zestful, Mr. Andersen has personally created the exceptional wine list that recently won the coveted "Best of Award of Excellence" from "Wine Spectator" magazine. For one of the finest dining experiences on California's Riviera, Claes' is a must.

Gravad Lax

1 1/2	*pound Norwegian or North Atlantic salmon filet, skin on*
1/8	*cup salt*
1/4	*cup sugar*
2	*tablespoons cracked black peppercorns*
6	*tablespoons chopped dill*
1/4	*cup Absolut Pepper Vodka*
1	*red onion, sliced paper thin*
12	*red "B" potatoes, cooked and kept warm*

Combine the salt, sugar and peppercorns. Place salmon skin side down in a deep container. Sprinkle liberally, using all the salt and sugar mixture. Top with chopped dill and layer the onions over the filet. Pour over the vodka and cover with plastic wrap. Place a heavy pan over the salmon, refrigerate and marinate for 2 days. Baste the salmon twice a day. Remove the filet and scrape all residue from the filet and discard. Wash the filet in cold water. With a slicer, thinly cut the salmon on the bias and serve with warm potatoes. The potatoes should be cooked in salt water until a knife can easily pierce the potatoes. Serves six as an appetizer.

Pavilion

Four Seasons Hotel
690 Newport Center Dr.
Newport Beach, CA
759-0808

Pavilion has been a consistent winner of the Travel/Holiday Award for fine dining and the Epicurean Rendezvous's selection as a member of the 100 best restaurants in Southern California. Recently, Pavilion received the California Restaurant Writers Association's Circle of Fame 4-Star award noting the restaurant as one of the top twelve restaurants in all of California. An elegant and extensive Sunday Brunch is considered the most elaborate and luxurious in Newport Beach. Dinner reflects the high standards that make the Four Seasons Hotels and Restaurants famous.

Grilled Scallops with Truffle Lobster Potatoes

Sauce:

2	*ounces olive oil*
2	*cups shallot rings*
1	*medium carrot, thinly sliced*
2	*bottles Pinot Noir wine*
1	*head split garlic*
10	*thyme leaves*
1	*bayleaf*
10	*peppercorns*
1/2	*gallon fish glace*
1	*pint demi glace*

In a hot pan, add olive oil and caramelize the shallots and carrots. Add 1 bottle of wine and reduce to sec. Add all the aromatics during reduction. Add the second bottle of wine and reduce until alcohol flavor is gone (3/4 reduced). Add fish glace and reduce by half to 3/4. Add the demi glace as needed for flavor. Reduce to desired flavor and consistency. Strain well and cool.

Lobster Truffle Potatoes:

5	*each large potatoes, skinned and diced (50 count)*
1	*cup lobster glace*
1	*cup butter*
1	*cup cream*
	salt and pepper to taste
4	*tablespoons crushed truffle*

2 cups finely chopped lobster
1 cup diced basil
1/2 cup chopped herbs

Cook the potatoes in salted water until just done. Drain well and puree until completely smooth. Slowly add the glace, butter and cream until desired flavor and consistency. Season and add truffles, lobster, basil and herbs. Cool and reserve.

3 per serving scallops, 10-20 count
3 truffle chips
1 diced tomato

Grill the scallops and cook until just medium. Split in half. Reheat the potatoes until thoroughly hot. To serve, put the potatoes in a small circle mold and center on the plate. Place the split scallops at 1, 2, 6 and 11 o'clock. Place truffle chips at 12, 4 and 8 o'clock. Add the sauce between the scallops and sprinkle with diced tomatoes. Garnish with basil flower.

HASSAN'S CAFE
3325 Newport Blvd.
Newport Beach, CA
675-4668

Hassan Hassan, owner and chef offers a rarity of a treat to us here in Newport, namely exotic Lebanese cuisine. A variety of old country dishes and those created by his own hand offer one of the truly uncommon and exceptional dining experiences to be had in Newport. Hassan's is open for lunch and dinner. Bellydancers grace the floor on Friday and Saturday evening.

Kafta be Akobbez
*(Ground Lamb with Onions and Parsley
in Pita Bread)*

6 6 inch Pita breads
1/2 pound fresh ground lamb
1/4 medium onion, finely diced
1/4 cup fresh parsley, chopped
  cinnamon

Mix lamb, onion and parsley. Season lightly with salt, pepper and a bit of cinnamon. Carefully open pita bread into two rounds. Pat 1/6 of the lamb on one side of each pita, covering the entire round. Close and bake in a 350 degree oven for 10 minutes. Do not overcook. Cut each round into four pieces and serve hot with Tahini sauce.

Tahini Sauce:

1/2	cup sesame paste
	juice of 1 1/2 lemons
1	small tomato, diced
	salt to taste

Add lemon juice a little at a time to the sesame paste, whipping until the mixture turns white and thickens. Garnish with chopped parsley, diced tomato and a sprinkle of cayenne and use as a dip for the Kafta be Akobbez.

GEN KAI JAPANESE RESTAURANT
3344 E. Coast Hwy.
Corona del Mar, CA
675-0771

Since 1980, owner and chef Hiroshi Toyosaka has offered authentic Japanese dishes such as sushi, sashimi, tempura, teriyaki and sukiyaki. The sushi bar is headed by Chef Taka Matsumoto, a native of Tokyo and a sushi chef for over 25 years. Gen Kai is open Monday through Friday for lunch. Dinner is served seven nights a week.

Kai No Sakamushi
(Steamed Clams)

10	littleneck clams
1/2	onion, chopped
2	garlic cloves, minced
1	teaspoon olive oil
1	tablespoon paprika
5	tablespoons Sake
1	tablespoon soy sauce
	lemon wedges
	pepper to taste

Put clams in light salt water for 30 minutes to get rid of sand. Saute onion and garlic in olive oil in a medium skillet. Stir in clams, Sake, soy sauce, paprika and a dash of pepper. Simmer covered until clams open, about 5 minutes. Stir occasionally. Serve with lemon wedges. Makes 2 servings.

PAVILION

Four Seasons Hotel
690 Newport Center Dr.
Newport Beach, CA
759-0808

Lobster & Frog Legs Wrapped in Phyllo

2	*1 pound lobsters*
1	*frog legs (3 per serving)*
1	*ounce Shiitaki mushrooms*
1	*ounce Chanterell mushrooms*
1	*ounce Morel mushrooms*
1 1/2	*teaspoons basil, tarragon, parsley, chopped*
6	*ounces lobster stock*
1/2	*ounce butter*
16	*sheets of phyllo*

Cook lobster in boiling water for 6 minutes. Remove and cool in ice water. Remove tail, arm and claw meat; chop into 1/2 inch chunks. Remove meat from frog legs. Saute in a hot pan in whole butter until 3/4 cooked. Slice the cleaned mushrooms into 1/8 inch pieces. Saute in a very hot pan in clarified butter. Mix the lobster, frog meat, mushrooms and 1/2 teaspoon of chopped herbs. Season with salt and white pepper. Lay out the phyllo dough, 1 sheet on top of the other (4 sheets total), brushing each sheet with clarified butter. Cut a circle in the phyllo about ten inches in diameter. Place about 3 ounces of lobster mix in the middle of the phyllo circle. Fold the phyllo up around the mix in pleats around the top to form a purse shape. Brush the outside with butter. Make 4 purses like this. Bake at 375 degrees in a convection oven until brown and hot throughout. To create the sauce, bring lobster stock to a simmer. Add the remaining chopped herbs. Season with salt and white pepper. Whip in the 1/2 ounce of butter. Place the strudels in the middle of 4 plates. Spoon the sauce around it, about 1 1/4 ounces of sauce on each. Garnish with chenille sprigs. Serves four.

SAPORI

1080 Bayside Dr.
Newport Beach, CA
644-4220

Sapori is located just before the bridge to Balboa Island. Chefs Franco and Andreano, brothers from Sicily, bring expertise in Italian cuisine that few restaurants can match. Sapori is open daily for lunch and dinner, offering dining in the gracious dining room or on the patio.

Manicaretto alla Palermitana

1	*eggplant, peeled, halved, halves butterflied*
1	*tablespoon garlic, minced*
1/2	*teaspoon fresh Italian parsley, chopped*
2	*pinches basil*
2	*tablespoons olive oil*
1	*fresh tomato, peeled and seeded*
	parmesan cheese

Drain water from eggplant with salt for 30 minutes. In a saute pan, saute eggplant, garlic, parsley and basil in the olive oil for 1-2 minutes. Add tomato and saute for another 5 minutes. Top with parmesan cheese. Serves two.

ANTOINE

Le Meridien Hotel, Newport Beach
4500 MacArthur Blvd.
Newport Beach, CA
476-2001

Antoine is no less than the finest French gourmet restaurant in all of Orange county. Additionally, according to the Ochsner Guide is ranked 15th in the entire United States. Executive Chef Jean-Pierre Lemanissier together with Master Consulting Chef, Gerard Vie of the Trianon Palace in Versailles, France have collaborated to create a menu that mixes French cuisine with contemporary flavors that will match the most discriminating in taste. The dress code is semi-formal and jackets are required by gentlemen. Antoine is open Tuesday through Saturday.

Medley of Fresh and Smoked Salmon, Mashed Potatoes and a Thyme Dressing

6	slices fresh salmon, 4 cm. x 6 cm.
6	slices smoked salmon, 4 cm. x 6 cm.
5	large potato, peeled and cooked
1	bunch chives, finely chopped
1	bunch thyme, finely chopped
1	bunch tarragon, finely chopped
1/4	cup cream
1	cup olive oil
	caviar and dill for garnish

Puree the potatoes and mix in the chopped herbs. In a double boiler, blend in the cream and slowly beat in the olive oil. Season to taste, cover and keep warm.

Thyme Dressing:

2	bunches thyme
1/4	cup chicken stock or water
	juice of 1 lime
1	cup olive oil

Blend the thyme with the chicken stock and lime juice. Slowly add the olive oil until creamy in texture. Salt and pepper to taste.

For presentation, pipe the mashed potatoes into the center of a serving plate. It should be approximately the same dimension as the salmon slices and 1 to 2 centimeters high. Lay a slice of smoked salmon on the potatoes. Season lightly and layer with a slice of fresh salmon. Place under a broiler for 1 minute. Do not overcook, the fish should be rare. Spoon a little caviar onto the center of the salmon with a sprig of dill. Trickle a little of the dressing around the plate and serve immediately. Serves six.

CAFE LIDO
501 30th. St.
Newport Beach, CA
675-2968

Located in the historic area of Cannery Village, Cafe Lido has the distinction of being one of the few real supper clubs in Newport. If you set out to design the perfect superclub, it would probably turn out like the Cafe Lido. The food, the music and the ambiance combine to make it an elegant and entertaining place to spend an evening. Open nightly and offering the best food and the best live jazz around, the Cafe Lido has become one of Newport's favorite gathering places. Here are two of its more popular and tasty appetizers.

New Zealand Cockle Clams

15	New Zealand cockle clams
4	tablespoons butter
1	garlic clove, minced
	marinara sauce as needed
2	ounces Pernod

Steam the cockles with water, butter and garlic until shells open. Drain from steamer. Top with marinara sauce and a dash of Pernod. Serve with garlic bread.

Oysters Felix

6	oysters
1/4	cup white wine
1	garlic clove, minced
1	teaspoon lemon juice
1	tablespoon shallots, finely chopped
2	tablespoons cream
2	tablespoons butter
2	egg yolks

Remove the oysters from the half-shell. Saute with garlic, lemon juice, butter, cream and shallots. Heat the empty half-shells under the broiler. Replace each oyster in its hot shell and pour pan juice over the oysters in each shell. Whip egg yolks in top of double boiler until fluffy, add butter slowly. Top each shell and add lemon juice and season to taste.

TUTTO MARE

545 Fashion Island
Newport Beach, CA
640-6333

Pomodoro e Mozzarella al Pesto
(Tomato slices with Buffalo Mozzarella and Pesto)

1   large beefsteak tomato, sliced
      fresh buffalo mozzarella cheese
1   tablespoon homemade or purchased pesto

Dress tomato slices with pesto and cheese.

STUFT NOODLE

215 Riverside Ave.
Newport Beach, CA
646-2333

The Stuft Noodle is one of the locals' favorite places to eat. Located just one block off Coast Highway, it is one of the best kept secrets in Newport. This cozy little restaurant has consistently been serving award winning Italian cuisine for the last twenty years. The owner, Robert Douk is always there to see that the service is just as warm and friendly as the dishes he offers. The Stuft Noodle is open daily for lunch as well as dinner.

Porcini Saute

1 1/2   pounds porcini mushrooms
1   ounce olive oil
1   tablespoon shallots, chopped
1   teaspoon garlic, minced
2   scallions, minced
1/2   ounce Marsala wine
1/4   ounce brandy
3   fresh basil leaves, minced
        black pepper to taste
1   cup beef broth
1   teaspoon butter

Saute mushrooms in very hot olive oil for two minutes. Add shallots, garlic and scallions. Saute for 1 minute. Add Marsala wine and brandy to flambe. Add black pepper, fresh basil, broth and butter. Cook for two minutes until smooth and serve.

RENATO

2304 W. Oceanfront
Newport Beach, CA
673-8058

After 30 years of experience in Italian and French cuisine including over 15 years at Maxim's in Paris, France and over 10 years as executive chef at Antonello's in South Coast Plaza, Renato Necci's dream of opening his own restaurant became a reality. Located on the oceanfront by the Newport Pier, Renato is the only fine Italian Restaurant in the immediate area. The restaurant offers an intimate European ambiance with efficient service and of course Renato's regard for fine cuisine. For a truly unique dining experience along with a romantic view of the ocean, a visit to Renato is a must.

Salmone Fresco Marinato

28	ounces Norwegian salmon
8	tablespoons clam juice
4	tablespoons extra virgin olive oil
3	tablespoons chopped fresh tarragon
8	tablespoons balsamic vinegar
1	teaspoon fresh basil
	salt and pepper to taste

Place salmon in a baking dish and poach over a low flame with the above ingredients. Cook for approximately 10 minutes until done. Remove salmon from the dish and cool. To serve, garnish with sliced fresh roma tomatoes, hearts of palms and artichoke hearts. Serves four.

THE TALE OF THE WHALE

Balboa Pavilion
400 Main St.
Balboa, CA
673-4633

Located in the historic Balboa Pavilion on the Balboa Peninsula, The Tale of the Whale offers fresh seafood and steaks. The view of the harbor is very spectacular and is one of the best places to watch the yachts heading out to sea. The Tale of the Whale serves breakfast, lunch and dinner daily.

Shrimp Scampi

1/2	pound peeled and veined shrimp
2	ounces soft butter
1/4	cup white wine
2	garlic cloves, chopped
	pinch of fresh parsley
	squeeze of lemon juice

Saute shrimp quickly in butter. Add wine, garlic, lemon juice and parsley. Reduce for two minutes. Do not brown. Serve with garlic bread.

NEWPORT LANDING RESTAURANT

503 E. Edgewater
Balboa, CA
675-2373

Newport Landing is located next to the historic Ferry Landing on the Balboa Peninsula. The view of the bay, coupled with great cuisine make this restaurant an excellent choice for any occasion. The downstairs Blue Room and Library show the more formal and elegant face of Newport Landing. Those looking for excitement and great live entertainment can choose the casual fun of the upstairs Oyster Bar and Lounge and outdoor patio. The fare is largely seafood, Hawaiian style. Newport Landing offers lunch and dinner daily, and brunch on Sundays.

Shrimp in Sherry Mayonnaise

1	cup mayonnaise
1	tablespoon dijon mustard
4	tablespoons dry sherry
1	garlic clove, minced
1	pound bay shrimp, finely chopped
	salt and pepper to taste

Combine all ingredients and mix well. Refrigerate for two hours. Serve over pumpernickel toast circles.

WATERCOLORS

Dana Point Resort
25135 Park Lantern
Dana Point, CA
661-5000

Watercolors is located in the exclusive Dana Point Resort that offers a spectacular view of the beautiful Dana Point Harbor. As the name implies, the decor is of soothing soft pastels. Together with a full view of Dana Point Harbor, the dining experience is one of tranquility. The menu offers a wide variety of Continental and California cuisines. Watercolors is open daily for breakfast, lunch and dinner.

Tortellini with Prosciutto, Basil and Dry Vermouth

1/4	pound fresh cheese tortellini, cooked al dente
1	slice prosciutto, cut into 1/8 inch strips
1/2	shallot, finely chopped
1	garlic clove, finely chopped
2 1/2	ounces dry vermouth
6	ounces heavy cream
1/2	plum tomato, diced
4	basil leaves, coarsely chopped
2	ounces grated romano cheese

Cook half of the prosciutto in a saute pan over medium heat for 1 minute. Add the garlic and shallots, stirring and cooking until the garlic is lightly brown. Add the vermouth and reduce by half. Add cream and reduce by a third. Add tomato, basil and remaining prosciutto and cook for another 30 seconds more over low heat. Serve on a plate. Ladle the sauce over the tortellini. Garnish with grated romano cheese.

NOTES

SOUPS, STEWS
&
CHOWDERS

SOUPS , STEWS & CHOWDERS

WOODY'S WHARF

2318 Newport Blvd.
Newport Beach, CA
675-0474

Located on the waterfront of the harbor, Woody's offers a wide variety of seafood and beef entrees. You can dine inside or on the screened and heated patio. For over 20 years, Woody's has been a favorite spot for dining and live entertainment nightly. Oh, if you are out on your boat, dock at Woody's guest slips and come in for a bite to eat and your favorite drink.

Boston Clam Chowder

2	onions, chopped
1	bunch celery, chopped
1	bunch leeks, chopped
1/4	pound butter
1	cup white wine
2	bay leaves
2	teaspoons thyme
2	cups water
1	cup flour
4	Idaho potatoes, peeled and cut up
16	ounces clams, chopped
16	ounces clam juice
2	tablespoons clam base
1	quart half and half
3	teaspoons white pepper
	salt to taste

Saute onions, celery and leeks in butter; when soft, add white wine, bay leaves and thyme. Saute for 2 minutes. Add water; bring to a boil and then add the flour. In a separate pot, simmer the potatoes for 12 minutes and add to mixture. Add clams, clam juice, clam base and white pepper. Boil for 10 minutes. 10 minutes before serving, add half and half and salt to taste.

FIVE CROWNS

3801 E. Coast Hwy.
Corona del Mar, CA
760-0331

Cock-a-Leekie

1 1/2	quarts chicken broth
2	cups leeks, julienne
1 1/2	cups chicken breasts, julienne
1/2	bay leaf
	salt and pepper to taste
8	stewed prunes
3	tablespoons parsley, chopped

Combine chicken broth, leeks, chicken and bay leaf; simmer 10 minutes. Taste for seasoning. Add prunes and parsley. Serves 8.

MAXI'S GRILLE

Red Lion Inn, Orange County Airport
3050 Bristol St.
Costa Mesa, CA
540-7000

Chilled Fruited Yogurt Soup

16	ounces plain yogurt
1	pint sliced, peeled ripe peaches
2	bananas, sliced
23	ounces apple juice
	juice of lemon
1/8	cup honey
1/8	cup orange juice concentrate
1/4	teaspoon nutmeg
1/8	teaspoon allspice
2	ounces peach brandy

Combine all the ingredients and fold in slices of fruit. Chill before serving. Serves four.

ANTOINE

Le Meridien Hotel, Newport Beach
4500 MacArthur Blvd.
Newport Beach, CA
476-2001

Cream of Lentil with a Celery Flan

1	celery stalk, coarsely chopped
1	carrot, coarsely chopped
1	onion, coarsely chopped
2	bacon slices
4	ounces lentils, soaked overnight
	bouquet garni (bay leaf, thyme, basil)
1	garlic clove
1	pint chicken broth or water
1	cup cream
1	chervil sprig
	salt and pepper to taste

In a large saucepan, saute the celery, carrot, onion, bacon and garlic until the bacon is crisp. Drain the lentils well and add to the vegetables. Add the chicken stock or water and bouquet garni. Simmer for 1 hour. Puree the liquid and pass through a fine strainer. Add the cream, season to taste and keep hot.

Celery Flan:

1/4	celeriac head, peeled and well cooked
1	egg
1/2	cup cream
	salt and pepper to taste

In a blender, puree the above ingredients. Pass through a fine strainer. Season to taste. Grease 5 small timbales and pour the liquid into molds. Cook "double boiler style" at 250 degrees in an oven for 15 to 20 minutes until the center is firm. Keep warm.

To serve, place warm flan in the center of a soup dish with a sprig of chervil on top. Pour hot soup into a tureen and serve hot at the table. An optional garnish would be a blend of finely diced tomatoes, carrots, onions and whole green lentils sprinkled around the flan. Serves five.

JW'S CALIFORNIA GRILL

Newport Beach Marriott Hotel and Tennis Club
900 Newport Center Dr.
Newport Beach, CA
640-4000

Located directly across from Fashion Island, JW's California Grill features fresh, innovative cuisine in a light, elegant atmosphere. The menu includes a festival of flavors through the creative use of exotic marinades and fresh herbs grown in the restaurant's own garden. Responsible for the menus, Chef John Michael Josberger offers diners a wide variety of choices, each with a delicious twist. The restaurant is open daily for breakfast, lunch and dinner.

Eggplant and Red Pepper Soup

Eggplant soup:

1	large eggplant, unpeeled and cut into 1/2 inch rounds
3	tablespoons olive oil
1	teaspoon chopped garlic
2	tablespoons chopped shallots
1/4	cup sliced onion
1/4	cup sliced sweet red pepper
1/4	cup seeded and diced tomatoes
1/4	teaspoon chopped fresh oregano
1/4	teaspoon chopped fresh thyme
1	teaspoon chopped fresh basil
	dash crushed hot red pepper
4	cups chicken or vegetable stock
1/4	cup white wine
	salt and pepper to taste
	chopped chives for garnish

Layer eggplant slices on oiled jellyroll pan. Brush lightly with 1 tablespoon olive oil and set aside. Heat the remaining olive oil in a medium saucepan. Add garlic, shallots, onion and red sweet pepper. Saute until tender but not brown. Add tomatoes, oregano, thyme, basil and crushed pepper. Spread evenly over the eggplant slices. Roast at 425 degrees for 15 to 20 minutes until lightly browned. In a food processor or blender, puree the eggplant mixture with half of the chicken stock, adding gradually. Return to the saucepan with the wine and remaining stock. Season to taste. Cover and let simmer for 20 minutes, stirring occasionally. Keep warm.

Sweet Red Pepper soup:

1	tablespoon olive oil
2	cups sweet red peppers, seeded and chopped
1	cup chopped onion
1	teaspoon chopped garlic
1/2	cup seeded and diced tomatoes
1/4	teaspoon paprika
2	cups chicken or vegetable stock
1	tablespoon brandy or to taste
1/4	cup heavy whipping cream
2	dashes hot pepper sauce
	salt and pepper to taste

Heat olive oil in a medium saucepan. Add sweet peppers, onion and garlic and saute until tender. Add tomatoes, paprika and broth and bring to a simmer. Add brandy to taste and simmer covered for 15 minutes. Puree pepper mixture in a food processor or a blender. Return to saucepan and reheat. Add the cream and hot pepper sauce. Season to taste and simmer until slightly thickened. Makes about 2 3/4 cups.

To serve, ladle eggplant soup into soup tureen or individual soup bowls. Top with red pepper soup to form a 2-tone effect. For marbleized effect, stir the soups in several quick strokes. Garnish with chives. Serves six.

MONIQUE

31727 Coast Hwy.
Laguna Beach, CA
499-5359

Monique is located on Coast Highway in the southern part of Laguna Beach. This cozy restaurant offers the finest in French cuisine available. Chef Guy brings to the restaurant the expertise and experience that has brought the restaurant numerous awards and recognition. If new to the area, Monique is a must for a genuine French dining experience.

La Soupe a la Farigoulette
(Artichoke Soup with Wild Thyme)

3	large artichokes
3	large chopped onions
6	cups water
1/2	cup short grain rice
1/4	cup extra virgin olive oil
1	bunch fresh thyme, stems removed except for 6 sprigs
1	cup whipped fresh cream

Boil the artichokes until leaves pull easily from the stems and drain. Saute the onions in the oil, adding the rice, water and thyme leaves. While the rice is cooking, remove the meat from the artichoke leaves and reserve. Clean the hearts and dice. Add the hearts, stems and leaf scrapings to the rice mixture. Cook the soup until the rice is tender, approximately 20 minutes. Serve the soup topped with whipped cream and a sprig of thyme. Serves six.

SCOTT'S SEAFOOD GRILL & BAR

3300 Bristol St.
Costa Mesa, CA
979-2400

Scott's is located across form South Coast Plaza, The Orange County Performing Arts Center and one block off of the 405 freeway on Bristol Street. Since 1976, Scott's has had a reputation few can match in the food service industry, a reputation for serving the freshest seafood, classically prepared, in warm, relaxed and inviting surroundings. Seasonally fresh seafood from local waters and around the world arrive daily. The chefs also prepare daily selections of poultry and meat entrees. A pleasant surprise is the variety of gourmet pizzas from Scott's custom oak burning oven.

Jambolaya

4	ounces chopped bacon
1	pound cubed ham
1	pound cubed chicken breast
1	pound Andoville or Polish sausage
4	ounces quartered mushrooms
2	diced red peppers
1	diced yellow pepper
2	diced green pepper
1	diced onion
1	8 ounce can chopped tomatoes in juice
1	ounce chicken bouillon cube or base
1/4	teaspoon cayenne pepper
1/4	ounce chili powder
1/4	ounce cumin
1/2	ounce oregano
1/4	ounce basil
	pinch rosemary
	dash rosemary
	dash tabasco
	salt to taste

Saute the bacon until crisp. Add the chicken, onions, spices and garlic. Saute until the onions are translucent. Add the remaining ingredients. Bring to a boil and cook for 20 minutes, stirring occasionally.

PAVILION
Four Seasons Hotel
690 Newport Center Dr.
Newport Beach, CA
759-0808

Lightly Spiced Corn Chowder with Smoked Shrimp

1	*small onion*
1	*small leek*
3	*jalapeno peppers*
1	*quart corn kernels*
2	*quart chicken stock*
4	*ounces butter*
12	*ounces whipped cream, stiffly whipped*
6	*shrimp (16/20 count)*

Saute the onions, leeks, jalapenos and corn in 1 ounce of butter. Cook until tender, do not brown. Add the stock, simmer and reduce to 1 quart. Blend in processor and strain through a fine chinoise. At time of serving, heat the stock until boiling. Place in the blender and add 3 ounces of cold butter and blend well. Place back in a pot on the stove and add whipped cream. Salt and white pepper to taste. Let boil until the cream rises up light and fluffy.

Smoked Shrimp Garnish:

On a small barbecue grill, smoke shrimp over coals and damp hickory chips until done. Peel and garnish soup.

DILLMAN'S

801 E. Balboa Blvd.
Balboa, CA
673-7726

Located in the heart of the Balboa Peninsula on the corner of Balboa and Main, Dillman's has a long history of serving the local residents and visitors. For over thirty years, Dillman's has been serving the best of seafood and beef. On "Wild Game Night" one can enjoy elk, venison, pheasant, or many other exotic game dishes. Dillman's is open daily.

Manhattan Clam Chowder

3/4	pounds bacon, diced into 1/4 inch squares
2	heads celery, chopped medium
5	onions, chopped medium
6	bell peppers, chopped medium
2 1/2	pounds of chopped clams
1	#10 can of diced tomatoes
1	#5 can of tomato paste
2	quarts clam juice
1	tablespoon granulated garlic
1/8	cup worcestershire sauce
1	tablespoon white pepper
1/8	cup salt
1/2	pound chicken base
1	pinch each of sweet basil, rosemary, and thyme

Saute bacon until crisp; drain bacon grease and set bacon aside. Add remaining ingredients to 5 gallons of water. Heat until boiling. Reduce to a simmer; cook until vegetables are tender. Mix flour and water to a smooth paste and add to soup to thicken to a medium consistency. Serves a crowd.

OYSTERS

2515 E. Coast Hwy.
Corona del Mar, CA
675-7411

Oyster Stew

1/4	cup whole butter
2	teaspoons garlic, chopped
1/2	teaspoon shallots, chopped
1	tablespoon red onion, diced
8	fresh shucked oysters
1/4	cup Chardonnay wine
1	tablespoon Anisette
3	ounces heavy cream
2	tablespoons corn kernels
2	tablespoons spinach leaf, julienne

In a large skillet, heat butter; add garlic, shallots, onions until half cooked and transparent. Add oysters and saute until oysters' edges curl. Add Chardonnay and cook out the alcohol. Add Anisette and clam juice. Turn heat to simmer, adding corn and spinach when vegetables are half cooked. Add cream, salt and pepper to taste. Do not let boil. Serve as soon as the cream gets hot. Serves one.

CLAES'

Hotel Laguna
425 S. Coast Hwy.
Laguna Beach, Ca
494-1151

Pacific Oyster Stew

24	*fresh oysters*
1	*diced onion*
1	*leek, white only, diced*
2	*stalks celery, diced*
1	*large russet potato, diced*
12	*ounces clam juice*
16	*ounces water*
6	*tablespoons flour*
6	*tablespoons butter*
1 1/2	*cups milk*
	basil, thyme and bay leaves

Shuck the oysters, dice and reserve the liqueur. In a large pot, saute the onion in the butter along with the leeks and celery. After 2 minutes, add the herbs and potatoes. After the vegetables are coated with the butter, add the flour, stir, then add clam juice and the water. Cook slowly until the potatoes are tender. Add the oysters with the liqueur and milk. Bring to a boil and remove from heat. Season to taste. Serves six.

MATTEO'S ITALIAN RESTAURANT

2325 E. Coast Hwy.
Corona del Mar, CA
673-8267

Matteo's celebrating over 20 years of service to the local community. From Avelino (Central Italy), this family serve dishes indigenous to the area as well as dishes from throughout Italy. The decor is one of warmth and intimacy. Matteo's is open for lunch Tuesday through Friday. Dinner is served Tuesday through Sunday.

Pasta e Fagiole
(Pasta and Bean Soup)

1/2	pound of mixed pastas, ie. shells, mostacciole, mafalda or fusili broken into pieces
2	tablespoons extra virgin olive oil
1/2	tablespoon fresh garlic, minced
1/4	cup onion, minced
1	15 ounce can of white cannellini beans or white kidney beans
4	cups chicken stock
1/4	cup marinara sauce
	salt to taste
1/4	teaspoon black pepper, coarse ground
1	teaspoon fresh parsley, chopped

In a separate pot, cook pasta in boiling water until done, drain well and set aside. In a medium sauce pan, saute onion and garlic in the olive oil until onion is clear. Add beans, chicken stock, salt, pepper and marinara sauce. Bring to boil, reduce heat to medium-low. Add pastas and simmer 10 minutes. Garnish with parsley and serve.

THE ALLEY

4501 W. Coast Hwy.
Newport Beach, CA
646-9126

Located at the corner of Coast Highway and Balboa Blvd., The Alley offers a menu of "American" dishes. However, Chef Jorge Guiterrez adds a "touch of Mexican" for flavor. Owned by Byron and Linda Kough, The Alley is one of those cozy little restaurants you will like whenever you need quiet, solitude, or intimacy. The Alley is open daily for lunch and dinner. Brunch is offered on the weekends.

Pazole Soup

2	pounds beef, diced
1	whole chicken, diced
3	pounds pork shoulder, diced
10	corn tortillas, cut into strips
1	teaspoon ground ginger
2	teaspoons oregano
2	teaspoons ground cumin
3	teaspoons chili powder
2	teaspoons coriander, ground
2	cups chicken base
2	jalapeno chilies, diced
2	small onions, chopped medium
2	stalks celery, diced
2	ounces lemon juice
3	carrots, peeled and diced
1	pound or 2 cans white hominy

Combine all ingredients, cook on low heat for 2 1/2 to 3 hours or until meat is done. Serve in soup bowl. Garnish with shredded lettuce, a square of cream cheese and 1 teaspoon of salsa and with tortilla chips.

GULLIVER'S
18482 MacArthur Blvd.
Irvine, CA
833-8411

Located across the street from John Wayne Airport, Gulliver's offers "the best prime rib in Orange County". The unique cooking process that was developed by founder Al Levie assures that the prime rib is far from ordinary. Their menu includes steaks, Wisconsin veal, duck and fresh seafood. Gulliver's is open daily for lunch and dinner. Brunch is served on weekends. Here are the recipes for two of their more popular soups.

Pea Soup

3	*ounces butter roux*
1	*cup diced onion*
1/4	*bay leaf*
1/2	*teaspoon nutmeg*
1	*tablespoon vegetable oil*
1	*quart fresh peas*
2	*quart chicken stock*
	dash white pepper
1/4	*teaspoon tabasco*
1	*ounce worcestershire sauce*
1/2	*teaspoon salt*
1/2	*teaspoon sugar*
3/4	*cup 40% cream*
3/4	*cup fresh peas*
1	*pint croutons*

Heat roux slowly in a double boiler and reserve. Combine the onions, bay leaf, nutmeg and oil in a kettle and simmer for 10 minutes. Add the peas and stock. Bring to a boil, reduce heat and simmer for 45 minutes. Add the pepper, tabasco, worcestershire sauce and sugar. Simmer for 5 minutes. Pass the soup through a fine sieve or puree until smooth. Return to kettle and bring to a boil. Add the roux and simmer for 20 minutes. Add the cream and bring to a simmer. Bring to a boil for 2 minutes and add the 3/4 cup of peas. To serve, ladle the soup into bowls and top with 2 teaspoons of croutons. Serves eight.

46

Potato Leek Soup

1/4	cup butter roux
1	cup diced potatoes
1/4	cup leeks, julienne
20	ounces chicken broth
20	ounces water
3/4	cup diced onions
3/4	cup leeks, diced into 1" chunks
2	cups diced potatoes
1	tablespoon worcestershire sauce
1	drop tabasco
	dash white pepper
1	teaspoon salt
1/2	cup whipped cream
	chives, finely chopped

Heat the roux slowly in a double boiler and set aside. Boil 1 cup of potatoes until tender but not mushy and set aside. Combine the broth and water. Cover the leeks with just enough of the broth and water. Bring to a boil and set aside to cool. Save the balance of the broth. Coat the bottom of a kettle with oil and saute the onions and leek chunks. Add 2 cups of potatoes and the balance of the broth to the kettle. Cover and bring to a boil for 10 minutes. Add the worcestershire sauce, tabasco, salt and pepper. Boil for 5 minutes more. Pass the soup through a fine sieve to puree the stock. Return to the kettle, bring back to a boil and add the roux. Cover and simmer for 10 minutes. Add the boiled potatoes and cream and bring to a simmer. Add the boiled leeks. Serve and garnish with chives. Yields one quart.

TETE A TETE

217 Marine Ave.
Balboa Island, CA
673-0570

Tete a Tete, a relatively new restaurant on Balboa Island offers the only French cuisine available on the island. The ambiance is cosy, quiet and intimate. Although a newcomer, this place has already won some major awards for its cuisine and service. For a romatic dinner with your significant other, Tete a Tete will definitely fill the bill.

Roasted Artichoke Soup

2	*medium artichokes*
1	*small sliced brown onion*
2	*tablespoons virgin olive oil*
6	*cups water or vegetable stock*
	salt and pepper to taste

To prepare the artichoke bottoms, break off the stem and using a very sharp knife, cut off all of the large leaves. Trim the base of any remaining green parts. Cut off the soft cone, leaving only the choke. Rub with a lemon and drop into a bowl of cold water with the lemon. Set aside. To prepare the soup, heat half of the olive oil in a large pot. Saute the onion and all the trimmings from the artichokes for 5 minutes or until soft but not brown. Add the water and season to taste. Simmer for at least 30 minutes. If necessary, add more water. Blend the soup in a blender and strain through a fine sieve. Return the strained soup to heat and reduce more if desired. To serve, slice the artichoke bottoms thinly and roast in the remaining olive oil until nicely browned. Place them on the bottom of soup bowls and pour the soup over the pieces. Garnish with chopped parsley or herbs. Serves four to six.

McCORMICK & SCHMICK'S SEAFOOD RESTAURANT
2000 Main St.
Irvine, CA
756-0505

This restaurant is part of a national chain headquartered in the Pacific Northwest. Consequently, many of the menu items have a distinctive bent toward the Northwest flavors and presentation. Executive Chef Joe Gonzales shares many of his own creations throughout this book. Be sure to try them. McCormick & Schmick's is open daily for lunch and dinner. Brunch is served on Sundays.

Seafood Chili

1	cup dry black beans
3	tablespoons olive oil
1	cup diced onion
1	cup diced red and/or green pepper
1	small jalapeno pepper, minced
2	teaspoons chipotle pepper puree (see note)
1	teaspoon cumin
1	teaspoon chili powder
1	teaspoon onion powder
1/2	teaspoon oregano
1/2	teaspoon salt
1	teaspoon black pepper
1	cup chicken stock, commercial or homemade
1	28 ounce can diced tomato
1	pound bay shrimp
1 1/2	pounds diced fish filets (cod, sea bass, rockfish, etc.)
8	ounces cheddar or jack cheese, shredded
1	bunch cilantro, chopped or sprigs
1	cup fresh tomato, papaya or avocado salsa
6	large flour tortillas, rolled and halved for garnish

Soak the beans overnight. Drain and cook in fresh water until tender. Drain and reserve. Heat 1 tablespoon of olive oil and add the next 10 ingredients. Cook over medium heat for 4 to 5 minutes. Add the stock and tomatoes, reduce heat to low and simmer 20 minutes. Heat the remaining olive oil in another saucepan and saute the seafood for 2 to 3 minutes. Add the chili sauce and beans to the seafood and cook for an additional 1 to 2 minutes. To serve, ladle the chili into bowls and top with cheese. Garnish with the cilantro, peppers, salsa and flour tortillas. Serves four to six.
NOTE: Canned chipotle peppers are available in specialty and Mexican groceries. Oriental hot chili paste also works.

JAMBOREE CAFE

Hyatt Newporter
1107 Jamboree Rd.
Newport Beach, CA
729-1234

The Jamboree features two distinct dining atmospheres; a relaxing and charming patio with a flowing fountain, or indoor bayside and garden views for breakfast and lunch. Dinner is served indoors, where the guests may dine in cheery greenhouse ambiance facing flower-filled red brick patios and Newport Bay. The light, airy undertones of the room carryover into the menu with colorful ripe fruits, crisp salads and different types of progressive California cuisine. The Jamboree is open daily for breakfast, lunch, and dinner.

Shrimp & Corn Bisque
in Bread Boule

2	pounds shrimp, 16/20 size, shell on
4	ounces olive oil
1	large white onion, medium diced
5	stalks celery, medium diced
3	carrots, peeled, medium diced
6	ounces brandy
2	cups white wine
1/2	cup tomato paste
1	tablespoon black peppercorns
6	sprigs fresh thyme
1	bay leaf
2	pints fish stock
2	ounces butter, melted
2	ounces flour
1	cup heavy cream
	salt and white pepper to taste
2	ears fresh corn, steamed and kernels removed
3	sprigs fresh parsley, chopped
6	6 ounce bread boules, hollowed out

Peel and vein all shrimp, save shells. Dice shrimp and put aside. In a soup pot, add oil; heat; add shrimp shells and saute until shells turn red. Add onion, celery and carrots; cook until vegetables start to caramelize. Add brandy and flame with a match. Add white wine and reduce by two thirds. Add tomato paste, herbs and fish stock and bring to a boil. In a small separate pot, blend butter and flour together and cook 5 minutes. Add to boiling soup and reduce to a simmer. Cook 30 minutes and remove from heat. Puree soup in a blender or processor. Strain through fine mesh strainer. Add back to a clean pot.

Place on stove and bring soup back to simmer. Add shrimp and cook 5 minutes until shrimp are done. Add heavy cream, season with salt and pepper.

Upon serving, place corn kernels in bottom of each bread boule. Ladle soup over corn in boule and garnish with fresh, chopped parsley. Makes six servings.

RISTORANTE CANTORI

Hyatt Newporter
1107 Jamboree Rd.
Newport Beach, CA
729-1234

Do you remember that special restaurant in Italy? It was only open for dinner, because it took them all day to prepare for that one perfect meal. Well, welcome back to Italy, at the Ristorante Cantori, featuring Northern Italian cuisine. Come sit al fresco watching the people pass by, with the sounds of a fountain playing in the background, or perhaps you would chose a table for two indoors with flickering candlelight. Whatever your preference for atmosphere, you will have plenty at the Ristorante Cantori. The decor and menu are Italian, right down to the bread sticks... and the waiters sing! Ristorante Cantori is open Monday through Saturday for dinner.

Stracciatella
(Chicken Broth with Spinach and Egg)

6	whole eggs
6	tablespoons fresh Parmesan cheese, grated
2	tablespoons fresh parsley, chopped
1	quart chicken stock or consomme
1	bunch fresh spinach, stems removed
	salt and white pepper to taste

Rinse spinach leaves under running water, pat dry, cut julienne and set aside. In a bowl, mix eggs, cheese and parsley, set aside. Bring chicken broth to a boil. While stirring, add egg mixture slowly and cook 1 minute until egg is cooked. Remove from heat. Add spinach and season with salt and pepper. Serve hot. Yields one quart.

NOTES

SALADS
&
DRESSINGS

SALADS & DRESSINGS

MARRAKESH

1100 W. Coast Hwy.
Newport Beach, CA
645-8384

Owner, Ali Rabbani has brought to Newport Beach one of the most unique edifices and menus in all the area. The Marrakesh has the appearance of a Moorish castle replete with towers. The cuisine is Moroccan, offering a rare and uncommon feast to our North American palates. Marrakesh is open for lunch and dinner daily.

Bell Pepper and Tomato Salad

2	large bell peppers
3	large tomatoes
1	teaspoon cilantro
1/2	teaspoon garlic, chopped
1/2	teaspoon cumin
1/2	cup olive oil
	juice of 1/2 lemon
	salt and pepper to taste

Bake bell peppers for about 15 minutes at 400 degrees. Peel while hot, remove seeds and dice. Put tomatoes in boiling water for one minute. Peel, remove seeds and chop. Put peppers, tomatoes and remaining ingredients in a bowl and marinate overnight.

BENIHANA

4250 Birch St.
Newport Beach, CA
955-0822

This chain of Japanese restaurants spans six countries. At Benihana, great American favorites like tender filets of beef, chicken and seafood are prepared according to a 1000 year old Japanese recipe. The Teppanyaki cooking experience allows your own personal chef to prepare your favorite meal tableside. This art of Japanese cooking uses the hibachi table as the chef's canvas. He is able to create his masterpiece in the tradition of harmony, where each ingredient complements the other, yet, in reverence to nature, each retains its own individuality. The result? "A work of art, satisfying both body and soul," as reported in Weight Watchers magazine. Benihana is open daily for lunch and dinner. Brunch is served on weekends.

Benihana Salad Dressing

1/4	cup chopped onion
1/4	cup peanut oil
2	tablespoons rice wine vinegar
2	tablespoons water
1	tablespoon chopped fresh ginger root
1	tablespoon chopped celery
1	tablespoon soy sauce
1	teaspoon lemon juice
	salt and pepper to taste

Combine all ingredients in a blender or food processor until almost smooth. Makes 6 servings. Unused dressing may be stored in a covered container in the refrigerator.

BLUE BEET CAFE

107 21st Pl.
Newport Beach, CA
675-2338

The Blue Beet is located across from the Newport Pier and has the distinction of being the oldest establishment in Newport Beach. The Blue Beet goes back to 1912. The fare at the Blue Beet is mostly fresh seafood, although steaks and chicken are available. On weekends, there is live entertainment. Stop by to relive a little history of the area, and enjoy a great meal. Open daily for lunch and dinner.

Blue Beet's Caesar Salad

3	garlic cloves, crushed
5	anchovy filets
3	tablespoons capers
4	egg yolks
1/2	teaspoon dry mustard
1	teaspoon Grey Poupon mustard
1/2	teaspoon black pepper
2	teaspoons worcestershire sauce
1/2	teaspoon salt
2	ounces vinegar
1	teaspoon sugar
10	ounces olive oil
6	ounces parmesan cheese

Place first 11 ingredients in a mixer at low speed until creamy. Slowly add the olive oil and the parmesan cheese. Refrigerate. Toss romaine lettuce in large bowl and slowly add dressing. Serve with croutons, fresh parmesan and garlic bread. Serves six.

THE ARCHES
3334 W. Coast Hwy.
Newport Beach, CA
645-7077

One of the oldest restaurants in Newport Beach (since 1922) and one of the most venerated, The Arches has won virtually every award a restaurant can win. For example, the wine list alone has received "The Wine Spectator's" Grand Award for one of the "Best 100 Wine Lists" in the U.S. for the past 5 years. The Arches is located at the intersection of Coast Highway and Newport Blvd., just across from the harbor. The cuisine is continental. Expect the best in service and personal attention. The Arches is open daily for lunch and dinner.

Caesar Salad

5	anchovy filets
1	garlic clove, crushed
1/2	teaspoon dry mustard
1	teaspoon worcestershire sauce
1	tablespoon vinegar
3	tablespoons olive oil
1	egg yolk
1/3	head romaine lettuce
1/2	lemon
1	cup parmesan cheese (Romano)
1	cup croutons

Crush anchovies and garlic in a small salad bowl and add dry mustard, worcestershire sauce, vinegar, olive oil and egg yolk. Stir until well mixed. Tear romaine lettuce in small pieces into large salad bowl. Squeeze lemon over leaves. Toss, add dressing; add cheese and croutons and toss again. Serves two.

JOHN DOMINIS

2901 W. Coast Hwy.
Newport Beach, CA
650-5112

John Dominis Restaurant on Coast Highway overlooks the Newport harbor. This restaurant is known for its lush tropical atmosphere featuring rich koa wood, lava rock ponds, waterfalls and muted flower fabric prints covering comfortable rattan chairs. Seafood is the specialty and there is always a large selection of fresh Hawaiian and Pacific seafood. Try the following recipe as it epitomizes what John Dominis stands for; grace, eloquence, style and class.

California Citrus Gravlax with Grapevine Smoked Vegetables and Dill Sabayon Sauce*

Salmon Gravlax:

1	6-8 pound whole Norwegian salmon
3	ounces Aquavit
1	ounce brandy
1 1/2	ounces lime juice
1	cup coriander seeds, crushed
1/3	cup white peppercorns, crushed
1/2	cup dill weed, chopped
1/2	cup salt
1 1/4	cup sugar

Filet salmon, leaving the skin on. Remove all bones from flesh of meat. Place skin down in shallow pan. Mix liquid ingredients together and marinate salmon for two hours. Drain 1/2 of liquid. Mix dry ingredients together and press onto salmon. Cover with plastic and place another pan on top. Place weights in second pan to press down and refrigerate for 72 hours. Lightly rinse and brush remaining salt and sugar off salmon. Slice into thin strands and make into roses.

Dill Sabayon Sauce:

1 1/4	anchovies
2	garlic cloves, peeled
1	shallot, peeled
1	teaspoon dry mustard
1/2	cup rice vinegar
2	egg yolks
1/3	cup peanut oil

59

1/4	cup sesame oil
1	bunch dill, chopped
1	tablespoon lime juice
	salt to taste
1	cup heavy cream
1/8	cup buttermilk
1/4	cup sweet white wine

Put anchovy, garlic, shallots, mustard and rice vinegar into food processor and blend until smooth. Add yolks and continue to blend while slowly adding the oil. Once smooth, remove from processor and fold in dill and lime juice. Add salt to taste and reserve in refrigerator. In a saucepan, combine cream, buttermilk and sweet wine on a low heat. Remove from heat, chill and place in a plastic container with lid and store at room temperature overnight. Fold into above mixture to finish sauce.

Smoked Winter Vegetables:

1	zucchini
1	yellow squash
1/3	jicama
2	carrots
15	snow peas, sliced
1	yellow bell pepper, sliced
1	red bell pepper, sliced
8	shiitake mushrooms, sliced
1	bunch green onions, sliced

Run zucchini, squash, jicama and carrots through a mandolin with fine blades (or slice julienne by hand). Mix sliced vegetables. Soak in 1/2 gallon of water and 1 cup of sea salt for 1 minute. Strain and smoke in smoker with either grapevines or desired wood until smokey flavor is obtained. Smoke in as cold a temperature as possible. Reserve.

Salad:

16	pieces baby red oak lettuce, washed
16	pieces baby red leaf lettuce, washed
16	pieces baby Boston bib lettuce, washed
16	pieces baby green leaf lettuce, washed
	(or use available winter lettuces)

60

Garnish:

1/2   *cup filberts*
8   *orchids*
1   *red bell pepper, sliced*
8   *leaves from red tea plant*

To assemble, place tea leaves as an underliner. Arrange lettuce leaves around salad plate. Place smoked winter vegetables in center. Arrange five salmon roses around plate and in center. Garnish with nuts, orchids and bell peppers. Serve Sabayon sauce on the side. Serves eight.

*Created by Executive Chef Robert Reash, Jr.

MARRAKESH

1100 W. Coast Hwy.
Newport Beach, CA
645-8384

Carrot Salad

8   *large carrots, peeled and sliced*
1   *tablespoon chopped cilantro*
1   *teaspoon cumin*
1   *tablespoon paprika*
1/2   *teaspoon chopped garlic*
2   *tablespoons sugar*
1   *teaspoon salt*
1/3   *cup white vinegar*
2   *tablespoons olive oil*

Boil carrots in water for 30 minutes, adding salt to taste. Let carrots cool, season with cilantro, cumin, paprika, garlic, sugar, salt, white vinegar and olive oil. Mix all ingredients together and marinate for at least 2 hours. Marinating overnight produces the best salad. Serves four.

THE CHART HOUSE

2801 W. Coast Hwy.   34442 Green Lantern
Newport Beach, CA   Dana Point, CA
548-5889   493-1183

The chain of Chart House restaurants has two in the area. One overlooks the beautiful Newport harbor while a second restaurant is on Dana Point bluffs overlooking the Dana Point Harbor. Nothing is more enjoyable than enjoying their fresh seafood or their prime rib as yachts sail by. The Chart House is open daily for dinner. Be sure to try one of their teriyaki dishes as they have given the sauce an unusual twist.

Chart House Bleu Cheese Dressing

3/4   *cup sour cream*
1/2   *teaspoon dry mustard*
1/2   *teaspoon black pepper*
1/2   *teaspoon salt, scant*
1/3   *teaspoon garlic powder, scant*
1   *teaspoon worcestershire sauce*
1 1/3 *cups mayonnaise*
4   *ounces imported Danish bleu cheese, crumbled*

In a mixing bowl, combine first 6 ingredients and blend 2 minutes at low speed. Add mayonnaise and blend 1/2 minute at low speed, then increase speed to medium and blend for an additional 2 minutes. Slowly add bleu cheese and blend at low speed no longer than 4 minutes. Refrigerate for 24 hours. Makes 2 1/2 cups.

CAFE 5-0-5

1109 Newport Center Dr.
Newport Beach, CA
640-5752

Cafe 5-0-5 is a San Francisco style cafe, located in Fashion Island. The cafe offers breakfast, lunch, and dinner on a daily basis. The menu tends to emphasize a lighter fare such as sandwiches and salads. Cafe 5-0-5 carries a modest but extremely adequate beer and wine list. Here is a salad that is quite popular with regular customers.

Chicken Fiesta Salad

	iceberg lettuce
	romaine lettuce
1	*red onion, sliced into quarters*
1	*tomato, sliced*
1	*grilled chicken breast, chopped*
4	*ounces cheddar cheese*

Fill a large bowl 3/4 full of lettuce at a 2-1 ratio of romaine to iceberg. Top with sliced onion. Surround lettuce with tomato quarters. The chicken can be purchased, however, fresh grilled is better. Top salad with chicken breast while hot. Finish with cheddar cheese so it can melt slightly. Add the salad dressing of your choice.

CLAES'

Hotel Laguna
425 S. Coast Hwy.
Laguna Beach, CA
494-1151

Claes' Salad Dressing

2	*teaspoons fresh tarragon, chopped*
2	*teaspoons fresh thyme, chopped*
1	*teaspoon fresh rosemary, chopped*
1	*teaspoon fresh oregano, chopped*
4	*tablespoons fresh parsley, chopped*
1/4	*cup red wine vinegar*
1/4	*cup rice wine vinegar*
1 1/4	*cup olive oil, pure or extra virgin*
	salt and pepper to taste

1   *pound mesclin lettuce or a variety of mixed lettuces, washed and drained*
1/2   *cup radichio, sliced very fine*
6   *1/4 inch thick slices of Montrachet Goat Cheese log*

Combine all the chopped herbs except for the parsley. Place the parsley, vinegars and salt in a blender and puree. Slowly drizzle in the olive oil. Remove from blender and add the herbs. Season to taste. When ready to serve, toss lettuce with dressing and place in the middle of chilled plates. Use the radichio to sprinkle around the border of the plates. Place 1 slice of goat cheese on each salad. Serves six.

DILLMAN'S

801 E. Balboa Blvd.
Balboa, CA
673-7726

Creamy Garlic Dressing

1   *gallon mayonnaise*
2   *onions, chopped fine*
6   *ounces garlic cloves, chopped fine*
1   *head parsley, chopped fine*
1   *bunch green onion, chopped fine*
1   *cup lemon juice*
1   *teaspoon white pepper*
1   *teaspoon granulated garlic*
1   *tablespoon worcestershire sauce*
1   *teaspoon tabasco sauce*
1   *tablespoon salt*

Combine onion, garlic, parsley, green onion and mayonnaise. Mix well.
Add rest of ingredients and add just enough water to achieve desired consistency.

MARRAKESH

1100 W. Coast Hwy.
Newport Beach, CA
645-8384

Eggplant Salad

1	large eggplant
1	cup olive oil
2	tablespoons cilantro, chopped
1	tablespoon paprika
1/2	teaspoon garlic, chopped
1/4	tablespoon white vinegar

Slice eggplant into slices 1 inch thick and fry in olive oil. Mash slices and season with remaining ingredients. Marinate at least 2 hours before serving.

MAXI'S GRILLE

Red Lion Inn, Orange County Airport
3050 Bristol St.
Costa Mesa, CA
540-7000

Georgia Peanut Salad

16	ounces field greens
8	ounces unsalted roasted peanuts
4	ounces pimento, julienne
8	each 6 inch flour tortillas

Wash the greens and gently toss with peanuts and pimento. Cut the tortillas into any decorative shape you desire. Brush with olive oil and herbs and bake at 350 degrees until crisp. Allow to cool. Toss salad and serve over the toasted tortillas. Serves four.

Dressing:

1/2	teaspoon salt
1	teaspoon mashed garlic
1	tablespoon fresh chopped tarragon
1	tablespoon fresh chopped chives
1	tablespoon fresh chopped parsley

1	teaspoon ground black pepper
2	tablespoons brown sugar
2/3	cup malt vinegar
1 1/4	cup peanut oil
2	tablespoons peanut butter

Combine all the ingredients and mix well. Allow it to age for 24 hours before using.

WATERCOLORS

Dana Point Resort
25135 Park Lantern
Dana Point, CA
661-5000

Grilled Shrimp with Young Greens

3	shrimp per serving, 16-20 count, peeled, cleaned, tail on
6-8	snow peas, blanched
1/4	carrot, julienne, 1/8" x 1/8" x 1 1/2"
	a mix of baby lettuce, cut, washed and dried

Dressing:

4	garlic cloves, finely chopped
3	tablespoons fresh ginger, finely chopped
10	ounces red wine vinegar
3	tablespoons oyster sauce
6	ounces sesame oil
6	ounces peanut oil
1	teaspoon ground black pepper

For the dressing, combine all the ingredients and blend slowly until the consistency is uniform. Grill the shrimp until done and cool in the dressing. Add the snow peas and carrots to the dressing. Toss the lettuce with some of the dressing and half of the carrots and peas. Mound the lettuce on a plate. Cut the shrimp lengthwise and arrange on the mound of lettuce. Garnish the salad with sesame seeds and the remaining snow peas and carrots.

RISTORANTE FERRANTELLI
25001 Dana Point Harbor Dr.
Dana Point, CA
493-1401

Located above the Dana Point Harbor, the Ferrantelli family has brought to the coast one of the finest restaurants of traditional and authentic Italian cuisine. Ristorante Ferrantelli originated in Rome, Italy in 1950. With over 40 years experience of preparing and serving Italian dishes, be assured only the finest ingredients are used in creating the exceptional menu. The wine list is extensive. Lunch and dinner are served daily.

Insalata Caprese

30	ounces mozzarella di bufula, sliced very fine
4	tomatoes, sliced
2	bunches sweet basil, coarsely chopped
12	tablespoons olive oil

Lay the cheese slices on a plate and top with the tomatoes and basil. Pour a desired amount of olive oil over the dish and serve. Serves four.

TUTTO MARE
545 Fashion Island
Newport Beach, CA
640-6333

Insalata di Afrumi e Capesante

3	ounces baby lettuce
1	ounce lemon, sliced thin
1/2	ounce orange, sliced thin
1/2	ounce grapefruit, sliced thin
	a few leaves of mint and fresh basil
1/2	ounce lemon dressing
	salt and pepper to taste
3	ounces scallops

Combine the fruits, lettuce and herbs. Toss with dressing and season to taste. Grill the scallops on the medium rare side to keep the centers moist. Serve with the salad centered on the plate and surround with the scallops.

ANTONELLO RISTORANTE

South Coast Plaza Village
1611 W. Sunflower Ave.
Santa Ana, CA
751-7153

Insalata di Pollo
(Chicken Salad)

4	*cups baby lettuce mixture, ie. arugola, mache, radichio*
4	*chicken breasts, sauteed or grilled, cut into strips*
4	*tomatoes, peeled and quartered*
1	*cup green beans and/or asparagus, cooked*
1/4	*cup parmesan cheese*
	extra virgin olive oil
	juice of 1 lemon
	salt and pepper to taste

Place lettuce into a salad bowl. In a separate bowl, combine the chicken, tomatoes and beans and/or asparagus. Drizzle the lettuce with olive oil until lightly coated. Add the chicken mixture and gently toss. Squeeze lemon over the salad and season. Serve and top with parmesan. Serves four.

Insalata di Tonna
(Tuna Salad)

4	*cups mache/arugola mixture*
8	*ounces fresh or canned tuna, grilled or sauteed in olive oil*
1	*tablespoon balsamic vinegar*
1	*tablespoon olive oil*

Place the mixture in a salad bowl and drizzle with oil and vinegar. Toss lightly. Flake tuna with a fork and toss gently with the greens. Salt and pepper to taste and serve. Serves four.

JAMBOREE CAFE

Hyatt Newporter
1107 Jamboree Rd.
Newport Beach, CA
729-1234

Lamb Salad

8	*ounces mixed greens, (butter lettuce, frisee, radichio, red leaf)*
1	*each red, green, yellow pepper, julienne*
2	*each roma tomatoes, julienne*
6	*ounces lamb tenderloin, cooked rare (see below)*
4	*ounces cabernet dressing (see below)*
4	*tablespoons Borsin or herb cheese, grated*

Place cleaned greens in bowl, add peppers, tomatoes and lamb slices. Add cabernet dressing and toss together. Place on plate and sprinkle top with cheese. Makes 2 servings.

Lamb tenderloin Marinade:

2	*cups salad oil*
2	*sprigs fresh thyme*
1	*bay leaf*
4	*heads garlic*
1/2	*tablespoon whole black peppercorns*
2	*sprigs fresh rosemary*

Put all ingredients in a bowl. Add lamb and marinate at least 6 hours before serving. At service, remove lamb and sear in hot pan until rare. Slice thin and add to salad. Toss with cabernet dressing.

Cabernet Dressing:

1 1/2	*cups salad oil*
1/2	*cup red wine vinegar*
1/2	*cup Cabernet Sauvignon wine*
3	*tablespoons sugar*
	salt and white pepper to taste

Mix all ingredients together.

FIVE CROWNS
3801 E. Coast Hwy.
Corona del Mar, CA
760-0331

Pride of the Crowns' Salad

1	teaspoon each, dry mustard, Lawry's Seasoned Salt, Seasoned Pepper and Pinch of Herbs
1	garlic clove, minced
1/3	cup red wine vinegar
1	cup olive oil
2	heads bib lettuce, torn into bite size pieces
3/4	cup walnut quarters
1/4	pound thick-sliced bacon, cut into 3/8 x 3/8 inch pieces, cooked until crisp
1/2	cup coarsely grated Gruyere cheese
1 1/2	cups croutons

In a tight sealing container, combine seasonings and vinegar; shake well. Add olive oil and shake again for about 30 seconds. Refrigerate several hours for best flavor. Then toss together remaining ingredients. Add dressing, toss again and serve immediately. Serves six.

THE WINE CELLAR

Hyatt Newporter
1107 Jamboree Rd.
Newport Beach, CA
729-1234

A tradition in Newport since 1969, The Wine Cellar has emerged as an exclusive and intimate dining retreat featuring French gourmet cuisine in the finest European tradition. The chef offers six prix fixe menus, rotated weekly. Each five-course menu features a choice of three different entrees. Open Tuesday through Saturday. Jackets required.

Salade de Haricorts Verts au Saint Andre
a la Creme d'Eschallots et Ciboulettes
(Green Bean Salad of St. Andre Cheese, Cream of Shallots, and Chives)

8	ounces mixed lettuces, butter lettuce, radichio, and red leaf
5	ounces Haricorts Verts (French green beans)
3	roma tomatoes
8	ounces Cream of Shallot dressing (see below)
8	ounces St. Andre cheese

Clean and cut lettuce into bite size pieces. Clean green beans and cut into 1/2 inch pieces. Blanch in boiling water for 1 minute. Rinse under cold running water. Dice tomatoes. Place lettuce in a bowl. Add green beans and tomatoes. Add dressing and toss. Divide salad on to four plates and garnish with pieces of cheese. Makes four servings.

Cream of Shallot Dressing:

3/4	cup shallots, chopped
1 1/2	cups sour cream
1/2	cup lowfat milk
1	teaspoon dijon mustard
2	teaspoons lemon juice
1	bunch chives, chopped
	dash worcestershire sauce
	dash tabasco sauce
	salt and white pepper to taste

Saute chopped shallots in small amount of oil until transparent. Set aside to cool. In a blender, blend sour cream, milk, shallots, mustard and lemon juice for 10 seconds. Remove and add chopped chives and season with the rest of the ingredients.

MONIQUE
31727 Coast Hwy.
Laguna Beach, CA
499-5359

Salade Mediterranean

2	pita breads, cut into 4 large slices
2	heads romaine lettuce, washed, dried, and broken into bite size pieces
2	chopped green onions
1	small cucumber, peeled, seeded and chopped
2	chopped tomatoes
3	sprigs fresh mint, chopped
6	sprigs fresh parsley, chopped
1 1/2	tablespoons sumac (a spice from the Middle East)
	juice of 2 lemons
3	ounces extra virgin olive oil
6	tablespoons feta cheese
12	Greek olives

Bake the pita bread until crispy and break into bite size pieces. Toss lettuce, onions, cucumber, tomato, mint, parsley and bread pieces. Add the sumac, lemon juice and olive oil. Salt and pepper to taste. Garnish with feta cheese and olives. Serves six.

ROYAL THAI CUISINE

4001 W. Coast Hwy.
Newport Beach, CA
645-8424

Exotic atmosphere and unique delicious food will be your fare when you dine at the award winning Royal Thai. The menu is extensive, featuring many authentic Thai dishes handed down through the Tila family for generations. Sam Tila and his six brothers all work together to bring you the best of Thailand. The Royal Thai is open daily for lunch and dinner. On Sunday, brunch is offered. For the real aficionado, Sam Tila, the owner, offers cooking classes.

Som Tam
(Green Papaya Salad)

1-2	garlic cloves
2	tablespoons Nam Pla
3	tablespoons lime juice
1	tablespoon Palm sugar, canned
1/2	pound green papaya, peeled, seeded, and coarsely grated
1/2	pound long string beans
1/4	cup salted dry shrimp, lightly pounded
1	tomato, sliced
1	head leaf lettuce
1/2	head white cabbage
2-3	green or red chilies, (Serrano)
1/4	pound cherry tomatoes
3	tablespoons peanuts

Blend garlic, Nam Pla, lime juice and palm sugar well. At serving, pour dressing over the papaya, sliced green beans, dry shrimp, sliced tomato, lettuce and cabbage in a mixing bowl, toss and mix well with dressing. Place the mixture on the platter topped with cherry tomatoes and peanuts.

THE GARDEN COURT CAFE

The Westin South Coast Plaza
686 Anton Blvd.
Costa Mesa, CA
662-6694

The Garden Court Cafe is located in the Westin South Coast Plaza Hotel. Recently, Chef Hans Loschl has created and designed a menu that reflects the wants and needs of today's society. The menu offers tasty, healthy gourmet cuisine yet not trendy. The Garden Court Cafe is just steps away from the Orange County Performing Arts Center and the South Coast Repertory.

Tabuli Salad with Oriental Dressing

2	ounces whole wheat, cooked until soft
2	ounces assorted baby lettuce
6	shrimp, blanched in salt water
1	ounce zucchini, julienne
1	ounce jicama, julienne
1	ounce carrot, julienne
	sesame seed

Combine all the ingredients and toss gently with the oriental dressing. Serves one.

Oriental dressing:

1	ounce fresh ginger
1/2	cup soy sauce
1/2	sesame oil
1	tablespoon plum sauce
	salt and pepper to taste
	sugar to taste
1	cup vegetable oil
2	sprigs fresh tarragon
1	garlic clove, minced
1	whole egg

In a stainless steel bowl, combine all the ingredients using a whisk. Season to taste.

PAVILION

Four Seasons Hotel
545 Newport Center Dr.
Newport Beach, CA
759-0808

Tomato, Avocado and Maui Onion Salad

1/2	peeled tomato
1/3	fanned avocado
2	small bunches lala rosa
1/2	ounce marinated Maui onion, see below
1	yellow tear drop tomato
1	ounce truffle vinaigrette

Thinly slice the tomato and fan. Roll into a tomato rose, leaving room in the center for Maui onion. Place the fanned avocado from center of the plate to 6 o'clock position. Place the tomato rose at 12 o'clock. Place the lala rosa bunches from center pointing to 11 and 1 o'clock respectively. Split the tear drop tomato in half and place at the center of the plate, covering the tip of the avocado fan and leaning off the tomato rose. Fill the center of the tomato with marinated onion. Ladle 1 ounce of truffle dressing over the salad.

Truffle Vinaigrette and marinade:

2	cups champagne vinegar
2	cups olive oil
3-4	cups salad oil
1/2	can crushed truffles
3	tablespoons chopped parsley
3	tablespoons chopped chervil
3	tablespoons chopped chives
	lemon juice to taste
	salt and pepper to taste
	truffle juice to taste

Put vinegar in a blender and put on high speed. Slowly add the oils to emulsion. Remove and place in a bowl. Add the remaining ingredients and season to taste. Slice a Maui onion thinly and marinate in the vinaigrette.

REUBEN'S

24399 Dana Point Dr.   251 E. Coast Hwy.
Dana Point, CA   Newport Beach, CA
493-8100   673-1505

This chain of steakhouse and seafood restaurants have long been a tradition in Southern California. Known for quality food, service and preparation, whether new to the area or a local resident, one can always count on Reuben's fare to be consistent and flavorful. Here is a long standing favorite among Reuben's customers.

Tomato-Shrimp Salad with Vinaigrette Dressing

12	ounces iceberg lettuce, broke into bite size pieces
6	ounces romaine lettuce, broke into bite size pieces
18	slices of fresh tomatoes
6	ounces bay shrimp

Combine the lettuces and serve 3 ounces each on six salad plates. Shingle each serving with 3 slices of tomatoes and top with 1 ounce of bay shrimp. Top each serving with 2 ounces of vinaigrette dressing. Serves six.

Vinaigrette dressing:

1	cup salad oil
2	tablespoons malt vinegar
2	tablespoons red wine vinegar
1	tablespoon worcestershire sauce
1 1/2	teaspoons dry mustard
1 1/2	teaspoons salt
1 1/2	teaspoons pepper
1	tablespoon finely chopped onion
1	tablespoon finely chopped parsley
1	tablespoon finely chopped capers
4	tablespoons finely chopped dill pickle

Combine the first 7 ingredients in a small bowl. Whip together to dissolve the dry mustard. Blend in the remaining ingredients. Refrigerate until needed. Yields 1 1/2 cups.

TREES

440 Heliotrope Ave.
Corona del Mar, CA
673-0910

Tucked away behind the Port Theater on Coast Highway, there lies one of the best kept secrets of the area. Trees is presided over by owner and chef Russell Armstrong. The cozy and romantic restaurant is comprised of three dining rooms with a piano lounge that surrounds an open air courtyard of giant Ficus trees. From their famous meatloaf with homemade mashed potatoes and Maryland style crabcakes to pasta, veal, lamb and an eclectic selection of dishes, Trees remains a major influence and trendsetter among the restaurants in the area. Getting there can be a little tricky, so be sure to call for directions if you are not familiar with the area. Trees is open daily for dinner.

Trees' House Salad & Tarragon Vinaigrette

1/2	head butterleaf lettuce
2	ounces Tarragon Vinaigrette (see below)
2	ounces bay shrimp
1	ounce roasted cashew nuts, chopped
1	teaspoon green onion, chopped

Wash the lettuce and drain (or spin) it well to dry. Remove the core and separate the outer (green) leaves from the inner (yellow) leaves. Arrange the lettuce in a floral pattern on a chilled plate. Place the outer leaves on the plate first, followed by the inner leaves, thereby, creating a pattern that moves from green outside to bright yellow center. Drizzle 2 ounces of dressing over the salad, distributing it evenly. Sprinkle with the shrimp and the cashews. Garnish with the chopped green onion.

Dressing:

1	whole egg
1 1/2	teaspoons salt
1/2	teaspoon white pepper
1	teaspoon sugar
1	tablespoon dijon mustard
2	cups salad oil
1/2	cup cider vinegar
1	tablespoon fresh tarragon or 2/3 tablespoon dried tarragon

Use an electric mixer with a wire whip. Place the egg, salt, pepper, sugar, and mustard in the bowl. Mix at medium speed until combined. Slowly drizzle in the oil in a fine stream while mixing so it emulsifies to make the base. This mixture should be thick and creamy like mayonnaise. Fold in the vinegar and tarragon. Adjust the flavor with salt, pepper and or sugar. The dressing should sit refrigerated at least one hour before serving to fully unlock the flavor of the tarragon.

FIVE CROWNS
3801 E. Coast Hwy.
Corona del Mar, CA
760-0331

Watercress and Mushroom Salad

3	tablespoons sherry wine vinegar
1	teaspoon dijon mustard
1/2	cup walnut oil
1/2	teaspoon salt
1/4	teaspoon pepper
2	bunches watercress (approximately 4 cups loosely packed sprigs)
3/4	cup mushrooms, sliced
1/2	cup walnuts, coarsely chopped
1/2	cup crumbled blue cheese
4	carrot curls, garnish

In a large bowl, combine vinegar, mustard, oil and seasoning. Add the remaining ingredients, toss lightly and serve immediately garnished with carrot curls. Serves four.

ENTREES MEAT

ENTREES MEAT

SHANGHAI PINE GARDENS

300 Marine Ave.
Balboa Island, CA
673-3802

Shanghai Pine Garden offers both Mandarin and Szechwan styles of Chinese cuisine. Located on Balboa Island, Shanghai Pine Gardens is open daily for lunch and dinner. After dinner, be sure to tour the island to walk off the generous portions they serve.

Beef Hunan

12	ounces beef, sliced
1/2	cup tapioca flour
2	whole eggs
2	tablespoons oil

Dredge beef slices in a mixture of tapioca and eggs. In a wok or saute pan, saute the beef slices in oil until golden brown.

Sauce:

2	teaspoons sugar
1 1/2	teaspoons vinegar
1	teaspoon lemon juice
1	teaspoon soy sauce
1	garlic clove, chopped

Combine sauce ingredients and cook in a teaspoon of vegetable oil. Combine an additional teaspoon tapioca flour and water. Combine beef, sauce and flour mixture and cook until thickened. Garnish with chopped green onion. Serves two.

ROYAL THAI CUISINE

4001 W. Coast Hwy.
Newport Beach, CA
645-8424

Beef Satay

1   *pound flank steak, thinly sliced*

Marinade:

1/2   *tablespoon curry powder*
1/4   *cup sliced onion*
1   *teaspoon roasted coriander seeds*
1   *teaspoon Nam Pra*
1   *teaspoon sugar*
1   *teaspoon oil*
1   *teaspoon butter or margarine*

Baste:

3/4   **cup coconut milk**
2   **teaspoons tumeric**
       bamboo skewers

Combine marinade ingredients and marinate beef strips for at least one hour. Grill on a barbecue. Combine coconut milk and tumeric. Baste skewered beef slices while grilling. Serve with satay sauce and cucumber sauce.

Satay sauce:

3   *cups coconut milk*
1/4   *cup palm sugar*
1   *tablespoon Tamarind sauce*
1/2   *cup peanut butter*
1   *teaspoon salt*
1   *tablespoon curry paste*

Combine all the ingredients and serve on the side.

Cucumber sauce:

1	*cucumber, sliced*
2	*green chilies, sliced*
1	*cup sugar*
2	*cups vinegar*
1	*teaspoon salt*
2	*ounces red onion, sliced*

Combine all ingredients and serve on the side with the satay sauce.

BLUE BEET CAFE
107 21st. Pl.
Newport Beach, CA
675-2338

Beef Stroganoff

1	*pound beef tenderloin, trimmed of fat, diced into bite size pieces*
1/4	*cup sliced shallot*
1/4	*cup sliced mushrooms*
1	*ounce brandy*
2	*ounces demi-glaze*
	sour cream

Saute the meat quickly at high temperature. Add onions; saute until brown in color. Add mushrooms and season to taste. Add brandy and demi-glaze. Stir well. Serve over pasta or rice and top with sour cream. Serves two.

PAVILION
Four Seasons Hotel
690 Newport Center Dr.
Newport Beach, CA
759-0808

Black Angus Striploin with a Four Peppercorn Crust

2   *8 ounce beef steaks, no fat*
2   *ounces four peppercorn mix; white, green, black and pink*
1   *ounce shallots, diced*
2   *ounces whiskey*
5   *ounces demi-glaze sauce*

Using a mixture of black, white, green and pink peppercorn, roughly crush them on cutting board with a pan. Coat the steaks with olive oil and roll in the peppercorn mixture. Season with salt. Saute in a medium hot pan in clarified butter and finish in the oven until medium rare. This will take 8-10 minutes. Turn the steaks often to insure even cooking. Remove from oven and let stand 5 minutes before slicing. Slice on an angle widthwise and arrange on a dinner plate. For the sauce, saute shallots in butter for 1-2 minutes. Add whiskey and reduce until all the liquor flavor is gone. Add demi-glaze and reduce to 4 ounces. Whip in 1/4 ounce of butter and season to taste with salt and white pepper. Garnish with sprigs of thyme. Serves two.

Tenderloin with Bone Marrow and Aromatic Herb Crust

4   *4 ounce beef tenderloin medallions*
        salt and white pepper to taste
4   *ounces bone marrow*
1/4   *cup finely chopped rosemary*
1/4   *cup finely chopped thyme*
1/2   *cup finely chopped parsley*
4   *tablespoons finely diced shallots*
8   *ounces fine bread crumbs*
2   *ounces whiskey*
5   *ounces demi-glaze*

Saute medallions in butter until medium rare. Season with salt and white pepper. For the crust, soak the bone marrow in ice water for 24 hours. Whip the marrow until smooth like butter. Add the chopped herbs and 1/2 of the shallots. Slowly mix in the bread crumbs. Add enough to create a nice cookable mix, not too greasy. Form into 1/4 inch thick patties and place over each medallion. Place under a broiler and brown well. For the sauce, saute the remaining shallots in butter. Deglaze with the whiskey and reduce by 3/4. Add the demi-glaze and simmer for 5 minutes. Finish with 1/8 ounce of cold whole butter. Place sauce on the plate with the medallions and garnish with thyme sprigs. Serves two.

Boneless Rack of Colorado Lamb with Pepper Herb Crust, Chive Mashed Potatoes and Vegetables

| 1 | rack of lamb, boneless and cleaned |

Pepper Crust:

1	pound fine bread crumbs
2	cups chopped herbs
3	cups crushed peppercorns, pink, green, black and white
	salt to taste

Combine all the ingredients and mix well.

Glace:

	Port wine glace from sauce below
	whole grain mustard
	lamb glace
	salt and pepper to taste

Combine all the ingredients in saucepan. Heat thoroughly and cool to room temperature. Season the lamb and roll through the glace. Roll through the bread crumbs, being sure to coat the lamb well and on both ends. Sear lamb in clarified butter and bake at 400 degrees for 10 to 12 minutes.

Sauce:

3	pounds lamb bones, cut into small pieces
10	finely sliced shallots
1	leek, white only, thinly sliced
1	finely sliced onion
2	stacks celery, thinly sliced
1/2	pound sliced mushrooms

peppercorns
bayleaf
thyme sprigs
2   *bottles port wine*
1 1/2 *gallons chicken stock*
1   *quart demi glace*

In a very hot pan, caramelize lamb bones 3/4 of the way. Add vegetables and caramelize the last quarter of the way. Degrease the bones and the vegetables allow to drain. Deglaze the pan with 1 bottle of port wine and add the herbs. Begin reducing and when the bones have drained well return to the pan. Reduce the port to sec. Add the second bottle of wine and reduce until the alcohol flavor is gone. Add chicken stock and demi glace. Reduce until flavor is good but not to strong. Strain and return to heat in a clean pan. Reduce to a glace and proper flavor. Strain and cool.

Chive Mashed Potatoes:

6-8   *potatoes, peeled and large diced*
1 1/2 *cups cream*
1   *head garlic, split (Cook with cream to make garlic cream.)*
1   *cup butter*
       salt and pepper to taste
2-3   *cups chopped chives*

Cook the potatoes in salted water until done, being careful not to over cook. Drain well and whip until completely smooth. Add garlic cream, butter and seasoning as needed. Mix in the chives.

Vegetables:

3   *pearl onions, peeled, blanched and seasoned*
3   *baby carrots, peeled, blanched and seasoned*
4   *asparagus, blanched and seasoned*

To serve, put 3 ounces of potatoes in a hot piping bag. On a plate, form a diamond with the potatoes, from 12 to 9 to 6 to 3 and back to 12 o'clock. Pipe the remaining potatoes at 12 o'clock for herb and potato garnish. Split lamb in 2 pieces, 1 larger than the other. Stand the longer piece at 9 o'clock and the other on its side at 3 o'clock. Arrange the vegetables at 6 o'clock. Ladle 2 ounces of the sauce over the lamb.

MARGARITAVILLE

2332 W. Coast Hwy.
Newport Beach, CA
631-8220

Margaritaville is known for its excellent Mexican food, but also offers great burgers and Caribbean specialties as well. At its circular bar, be sure to try their margaritas, as it was recently awarded the distinction of serving the best margarita in Orange County or Los Angeles County. Margaritaville is open daily for lunch and dinner.

Carne Asada
(Mexican Marinated Steak)

1   ounce New York steak

Marinade:

juice of 4 oranges
juice of 4 limes
1/2   cup salad oil
oregano, enough to cover both sides of the steak
salt and pepper to taste

Combine all the ingredients in a shallow baking pan. Baste steak in the mixture and cover both sides with generous amount of oregano. Marinate for two hours. Broil steak over hot mesquite coals.

OPASO'S BALBOA THAI CAFE
209 1/2 Palm St.
Balboa, CA
675-0161

In the heart of the Balboa Fun Zone is an unassuming place, off the beaten path, called Opaso's. This cozy and intimate establishment offers one of the more intriguing menus in the Newport area. If you enjoy oriental food, especially from Thailand, Opaso's is a must. They are open daily for dinner except on Mondays.

Chili Beef

1 1/2	*tablespoons salad oil*
1-2	*garlic cloves, minced*
2-3	*pieces fresh chili peppers*
1/2	*cup sliced fresh vegetables, ie. green onions, string beans, asparagus, mushrooms, eggplant or broccoli*
8	*ounces beef tenderloin, thinly sliced*
2-3	*tablespoons chicken stock*
2	*teaspoons soy sauce*
1	*pinch brown sugar*
1	*bunch fresh basil or mint, chopped*
	salt to taste

Heat wok with salad oil. Add garlic and peppers. Fry until brown. Add vegetables, cook down and add beef and seasonings. After beef is done, add basil or mint. Serve with steamed rice and fresh fruit. Makes one serving.

ROYAL THAI CUISINE
4001 W. Coast Hwy.
Newport Beach, CA
645-8424

Crying Tiger

1	*10 ounce prime cut steak*
1/2	*teaspoon white pepper*
2	*tablespoons oil*

Marinate beef with oil and pepper for 1-2 hours. Grill beef until medium rare. Slice beef into pieces and place onto lettuce leaves.

Sauce for dipping:

1/4	cup finely chopped shallots
1	tablespoon dry chili powder
2	tablespoons lime juice
1/2	teaspoon sugar
1/2	tablespoon Nam pla
1/2	tablespoon Maggi sauce
1	pinch green onion, chopped

Mix shallots, chili powder, Nam pla, Maggi sauce, sugar and green onion. Stir until well mixed. Garnish with cabbage, lettuce, green onion or cilantro.

SAPORI
1080 Bayside Dr.
Newport Beach, CA
644-4220

Filetto di Bue al Barbaresco e Porcini
(Tenderloin Sauteed with Cognac in a Barbaresco Sauce with Porcini)

1	8 ounce beef tenderloin
1/2	tablespoon butter, clarified
1	tablespoon olive oil
1	ounce cognac
1 1/2	cups sliced porcini mushrooms
1	carrot, peeled and chopped
1	green onion, chopped
1	stalk celery, chopped
1	garlic clove, chopped
1/2	teaspoon thyme
3	bay leaves
1 1/2	cup Barbaresco wine

In a heavy pan, saute the tenderloin in clarified butter and olive oil. Add cognac and set beef aside. Add mushrooms, chopped vegetables, garlic, thyme and bay leaf, saute until vegetables are soft. Add Barbaresco wine, cook down to thicken. Add the tenderloin, salt and pepper to taste.

HASSAN'S CAFE
3325 Newport Blvd.
Newport Beach, CA
675-4668

Kafta Be Sineeya

1	pound ground lamb
1/4	bunch parsley, chopped
1/2	small brown onion, chopped fine
	salt and pepper to taste
2	potatoes, diced
2	tomatoes, sliced
8	ounces tomato paste
	dash of cinnamon

Mix in a bowl, the lamb, parsley, onions and salt and pepper. Make small patties and put in a casserole dish. Place potato slices, then place tomato slices over the potatoes and patties. Mix the paste with 1 1/2 cans of water. Pour over the casserole with a dash of cinnamon and a little margarine. Cover and bake for 30 minutes at 350 degrees. Serve with rice or pasta.

THE ALLEY

4501 W. Coast Hwy.
Newport Beach, CA
646-9126

Lamb Shank, Marinated

1	lamb shank
2	tablespoons salt
1	cube butter
1	stalk celery, chopped
6	carrots, peeled and sliced
3	onions, diced
2	tablespoons beef base
2	ounces lemon juice
2	bunches fresh mint, chopped
1-2	whole apples
3	bay leaves
1	teaspoon thyme
2	teaspoons sweet basil
2	teaspoons marjoram
2	teaspoons tarragon
2	teaspoons cut dillweed
2	teaspoons whole fennel seed
1/2	gallon burgundy wine
2	tablespoons garlic cloves, crushed
1/2	gallon water

Combine all the marinade ingredients and mix thoroughly. Marinate the shank for 6-8 hours. Roast in oven 2 1/2 to 3 hours at 400 degrees. Serves ten.

PAVILION
Four Seasons Hotel
690 Newport Center Dr.
Newport Beach, CA
759-0808

Loin of Rabbit with Braised White Cabbage and Madeira Sauce

2	*rabbits*
1/2	*head white cabbage, sliced 1/4 inch thick*
1/4	*cup minced onions*
1/4	*cup minced bacon*
1	*quart jus de poulet or double chicken stock*
8	*ounces madeira sauce*

Bone rabbits saving the loins for preparation. Save leg meat for another recipe. Chop the carcass in small pieces. Brown off the bones in a very hot rondeau in olive oil. Brown until very crisp. Drain off the excess fat. Deglaze with the madeira. Reduce the madeira until dry. Add the jus de poulet and simmer. Reduce to about 4 ounces and strain through a fine chinoise. Saute the rabbit loins in clarified butter and season with salt and white pepper. Cook as chicken, until cooked throughout but still moist.

In a separate pan, saute the bacon until 3/4 crisp, add onions and finish the bacon. Drain off the excess fat and add the cabbage. Add 1 ounce of rabbit stock and cook until tender. When cooked drain off the excess juice. Place cabbage in an oval mold on a dinner plate. Slice the rabbit loins widthwise about 9-10 slices each. Fan 1 loin around each side of the cabbage. For the sauce, boil the strained stock and whip in 1/2 ounce cold butter. Season to taste. Spoon 2 ounces over the rabbit. Garnish with diced tomato and thyme sprigs.

THE QUIET WOMAN

3224 E. Coast Hwy.
Corona del Mar, CA
640-7440

Established in 1965, the Quiet Woman is a favorite spot of the local residents. Tucked away behind ivy covered bricks, the friendly, casual atmosphere and simply great food keep the waiting list full almost every night. The Quiet Woman specializes in rack of lamb, baseball steaks and thick cut swordfish. Stop in for a cocktail, stay for dinner, spend the evening listening to some very talented musicians.

Marinated Pork Chops

4   center cut, frenched, loin chops, 3/4 to 1 inch thick

Marinade:

3/4   cup plum sauce
1 1/2   cups hoisen sauce
1/4   cup soy sauce
1/2   bottle rice wine vinegar (12.7 ounce bottle)
1   tablespoon fresh minced garlic
1/2   tablespoon fresh grated ginger
1/4   teaspoon black pepper
1   tablespoon ketchup
1 1/2   cups black bean paste

For the black bean paste, simmer black beans in water with garlic until reduced to a thick soup like or paste consistency. Start with 1 part beans to 1 part water and add more water a bit at a time as needed. It will take several hours to reach the thickness required. The paste can be made ahead of time and refrigerated or frozen.

Mix all the ingredients together in a shallow container. Add the pork chops, spooning the marinade over the top. Marinate for 12 hours and turn the chops. The chops should be chargrilled or charbroiled to an internal temperature of 160 degrees. Serves four.

RENATO

2304 W. Oceanfront
Newport Beach, CA
673-8058

Medaglioni di Vitello Diana
(Veal Medallions Diana)

8	4 ounce veal filets
4	teaspoons chopped shallots
12	sliced mushrooms
1	ounce dry white wine
1	ounce beef bouillon
4	teaspoons dry dijon mustard
4	tablespoons heavy whipping cream

Grill the filets until medium rare over a medium flame. Combine the remaining ingredients and saute the filets in the mixture over medium flame until done to desired rareness. Serves four.

CIAO MEIN

Hyatt Regency, Irvine
17900 Jamboree
Irvine, CA
975-1234

As the restaurant's name implies, the Hyatt Regency has made a daring move in creating one of the more unique restaurants in the area, offering both Chinese and Italian cuisine. Executive Chef Steve Tresvik has put together a formidable team of chefs that will assure any person this relatively new restaurant will be a serious contender for any upcoming culinary honors.

Mongolian Beef

7	ounces top sirloin, cut into 1" strips

Marinade:

6	tablespoons water
4	whole eggs
2	tablespoons cornstarch
4	tablespoons salad oil
1	teaspoon baking soda
	salt and pepper to taste

Combine the above ingredients and marinate the top sirloin for at least 8 hours.

2	ounces bell peppers, julienne
1	ounce slice bamboo
1	ounce white onion, julienne
1/2	teaspoon minced garlic
1/2	teaspoon minced ginger
1/2	teaspoon chili paste
2	tablespoons white wine
1	ounce sesame oil
1	tablespoon cornstarch
2	cups frying oil
5	ounces Mongolian sauce (see below)
	salt and pepper to taste
3	cilantro leaves per serving

Fry the beef in hot oil for 1 to 2 minutes, then drain. Heat a wok with about 2 tablespoons of oil and saute the peppers, bamboo and onion. When soft, thicken with 1/4 teaspoon cornstarch and set aside. Quickly rinse the wok and heat again with 1 teaspoon of oil. Saute the ginger and garlic with the chili paste. Add the wine and Mongolian sauce. Boil, add cornstarch, then sesame oil and quickly toss in the beef. Toss several times, season to taste and place over the pepper mixture. Garnish with the cilantro leaves. Serves one.

Mongolian sauce:

1/2   cup ketchup
1/2   cup A-1 sauce
1/2   cup worcestershire sauce
1/2   cup Maggi seasoning
1/2   cup hoisin
       sugar to taste

Combine all the ingredients.

MARRAKESH

1100 W. Coast Hwy.
Newport Beach, CA
645-8384

Moroccan Couscous

1   pound lamb, cubed
1   large chicken breast, boned, skinned and cubed
2   carrots, peeled and cut in chunks
1   onion, chopped
1   8 ounce can garbanzo beans, drained
2   tablespoons olive oil
4   tablespoons butter or margarine
3   quarts water
1   tablespoon salt
       generous pinch of saffron
1/2   teaspoon coarse black pepper
2   cups couscous (available at specialty stores)
1   small zucchini, cut in 1/2 inch pieces
1   small turnip, peeled and coarsely chopped
1   tomato, peeled and chopped
1/2   small cabbage, quartered

2-3   sprigs parsley, chopped
1/2   small bunch cilantro, chopped
1/2   cup raisins

In a kettle, combine lamb, chicken, carrots, onion, garbanzo beans, olive oil, 2 tablespoons butter and water. Add salt and saffron (pounded together in a mortar) and pepper. Bring to boil and simmer 15 minutes. Carefully remove 2 cups hot broth and add to couscous in a large saucepan. Add remaining butter and stir carefully so grains remain separate and can swell evenly. Cover and keep hot 15-20 minutes. (Do not place over heat.) Add more broth, if needed. Grains should be fluffy, not gummy when finished. Simmer meat and vegetables an additional 15 minutes, then add zucchini, turnip, tomato, cabbage, parsley, cilantro and raisins. Cook about 25 minutes or until cabbage and turnip are tender. Place couscous in a large serving dish and fluff the grains with two forks. Arrange drained meat and vegetables over couscous. Serve broth separately to be poured over servings. Serves 8-10.

THE QUIET WOMAN

3224 E. Coast Hwy.
Corona del Mar, CA
640-7440

New York Pepper Steak

4   New York steaks
1/2   cup chopped morel mushrooms
2 1/4 teaspoons minced fresh garlic
3   tablespoons butter
1/2   teaspoon flour
1/2   cup beef consomme
2 1/2 tablespoons cooking sherry
1   red bell pepper, diced and seeded
1   green bell pepper, diced and seeded
2   dozen white mushroom caps
1   small yellow onion, diced
4   stalks chopped green onions
1   dozen green peppercorns, crushed
1/4   cup black peppercorns, crushed

Morel mushroom sauce:

Saute morel mushrooms in 1 tablespoon of butter and 1/4 teaspoon garlic for 10 minutes on low heat. Remove the mushrooms. Add flour to butter to make a roux. Add sauted mushrooms, the consomme and 2 tablespoons sherry. Stir and bring to boil, cook until sauce thickens. Set aside.

Pepper saute:

In a large saute pan, melt 2 tablespoons butter, add 1/4 teaspoon garlic and 1/4 cup sherry. Add all diced and chopped vegetables and green peppercorns (green only). Add only 8 whole white mushroom caps. Saute over low heat until onion is translucent and pepper is soft.

Rub remainder of garlic into the steaks. Coat the steaks with the black peppercorns. Charbroil the steaks. To serve, spoon the morel mushroom sauce onto the plate placing the steak on top. Spoon pepper saute on the steak and garnish with two white mushrooms. Serves four.

GEN KAI
3344 E. Coast Hwy.
Corona del Mar, CA
675-0771

New York Steak, Japanese Style

1   7-10 ounce New York steak

Marinade:

1   tablespoon mirin (Japanese sweet cooking sake)
1   tablespoon sake
2   tablespoon soy sauce

Marinate steak in for 7 to 8 minutes. Cook steak to preference.

Sauce:

2	tablespoons rice vinegar
2	teaspoons soy sauce
2	teaspoons mirin
5	tablespoons grated daikon (white radish)
1	tablespoon green onion, finely chopped
1	garlic clove, grated
1/4	onion, grated

Combine vinegar, soy sauce and mirin. Add garlic, onion, green onion and daikon. Cook just enough for it to warm. Pour over steak. Serves one.

RISTORANTE CANTORI

Hyatt Newporter
1107 Jamboree Rd.
Newport Beach, CA
729-1234

Osso Bucco Romano
(Roasted Veal Shank)

6	veal shanks
	salt and pepper to taste
1	cup flour
4	ounces olive oil
1	onion, medium dice
4	stalks celery, medium dice
2	carrots, medium dice
2	zucchini, medium dice
1	tablespoon garlic, chopped
1/2	tablespoon shallots, chopped
6	roma tomatoes, medium dice
1/2	cup tomato paste
1 1/2	cups red wine
1/2	cup white wine
2	quarts veal stock

Tie the following in cheese cloth:

2	*sprigs fresh rosemary*
3	*bay leaves*
3	*sprigs fresh thyme*
1	*tablespoon black peppercorns*

Season veal with salt and black pepper and dust with flour. In a large pan, add olive oil and heat.   Sear veal on both sides until golden. Remove and set aside. In same oil, add onion, celery, carrot and saute 2 minutes. Add zucchini, garlic, shallots, tomatoes and tomato paste. Saute another 2 minutes. Add veal back to pan with vegetables. Add red and white wines and reduce two thirds. Add veal stock and herbs in cheesecloth; cover pot, and place in 350 degree oven for 1 1/2 hours, or until veal is fork tender. When done, remove meat from pan. Set aside and keep warm. Put pan back on and reduce until sauce thickens to consistency (until it coats the spoon). Season and strain sauce through fine sieve. Place veal on plate and pour sauce over veal.

THE DINING ROOM

The Ritz-Carlton
33533 Ritz-Carlton Dr.
Dana Point, CA
240-2000

The Ritz-Carlton is considered by many as the premiere flagship of the Riviera's resorts. It sits on the north bluff of Dana Point overlooking the Pacific Ocean. The majestic view is only matched by the creations of Executive Chef Christian Rassinoux. The menu of "The Dining Room" is varied and eclectic. Cuisine is international in flavor, California in presentation and superb in preparation. For those who truly have a love of gourmet dining, "The Dining Room" is not a place to be missed.

Petit Chausson of Braised Rabbit with White Baby Onions in Honey, Thyme and Merlot Vinegar Reduction

1	*rabbit*
20	*peeled baby white onions*
3	*ounces bacon*
2	*tablespoons honey*
1	*small bouquet garni (fresh thyme, 2 fresh bayleaves and 1 small sprig tarragon)*
4	*whole garlic cloves, chopped*
2	*ounces olive oil*
1/3	*cup aged red wine vinegar*
1 1/2	*cups Merlot wine*

100

1/3   cup white stock
       cracked pepper and salt
       ravioli

Cut the rabbit into 6 to 8 pieces and season with salt and pepper. In a hot pan, add olive oil and saute the rabbit until golden brown. Remove from pan. Saute the bacon, onions and garlic. Add the rabbit and vinegar and cook to a glaze. Add the stock, the honey and the bouquet garni. Cook over low heat until the meat falls from the bones. Remove the rabbit and bouquet garni. Remove all bones and chop the meat roughly. Strain the garnish from the sauce. Roughly chop the bacon and onions, return to the sauce and cook for 3 minutes. Remove from heat and let cool. Mix half of the sauce with garnish and the rabbit meat. Stuff into ravioli. Bake in the oven. Before serving, make an incision on the top and garnish with the pearl onion compote.

CARMELO'S RISTORANTE ITALIANO

3520 E. Coast Hwy.
Corona del Mar, CA
675-1922

Superb Italian cuisine and attentive Continental service makes an evening a special occasion. The menu is large and varied; pastas, seafood, chicken, beef and veal. One of Carmelo's specialties is the filet mignon stuffed with fontina cheeses and prosciutto, topped with fresh mushrooms. Carmelo's is opened nightly for dinner.

Saltimbocca alla Romana
(Veal Scallops with Prosciutto and Sage)

12   veal scallops
6   slices prosciutto
12   fresh sage leaves
1   tablespoon butter
1/2   cup white wine
      salt and fresh ground pepper

Place 1/2 slice of prosciutto and a sage leaf on each veal slice. Roll up each piece and secure with a toothpick. Melt the butter in a heavy skillet and brown the veal rolls well. Add the white wine and cook until reduced to several tablespoons, scraping the browned bits from the bottom of the pan. Cover and cook over low heat for 20 minutes, adding water a tablespoon or so at a time to keep meat from drying out. Serve rolls hot.

THE OLD DANA POINT CAFE
24720 Del Prado Ave.
Dana Point, CA
661-6003

As the name implies, The Old Dana Point Cafe is located in a building that is close to 75 years old. The restaurant offers a California cuisine and has one of the few wine bars in the area. Lunch and dinner are served daily with a brunch on weekends. Patio dining is also available. There is nightly entertainment as well.

Southwestern Meat Loaf

1/2	cup cornmeal
1/2	cup tomato juice
1	tablespoon olive oil
1	small red onion, chopped
1/4	cup fresh cilantro, chopped
2	large garlic cloves, chopped
1	teaspoon salt
1	pound ground beef
1/2	pound ground pork
1	egg
1	tablespoon chili powder
1	tablespoon cumin
1	minced jalapeno pepper
1	avocado, peeled and sliced

Whisk cornmeal into the tomato juice and let stand. Heat olive oil in a skillet and saute the onion, cilantro, garlic and salt. Stir until the cilantro "melts", about 2 minutes and let cool. Combine the ground meats and knead into the cornmeal and onion mixture. Beat the egg and combine with the chili powder, cumin and jalapeno. Add this to the meat and mix very well. Pack a loaf into a lightly greased loaf pan. Cover with foil and bake at 350 degrees for 30 minutes. Remove the foil and bake at 400 degrees for an additional 30 minutes. Serve with baked potato and vegetable. Garnish with avocado slices and sprigs of cilantro. Serves six.

THE ARCHES

3334 W. Coast Hwy.
Newport Beach, CA
645-7077

Steak Diane

2	New York steaks
1/4	cup butter
2	teaspoon shallots, crushed
2	cups mushrooms, sliced
1/4	teaspoon cracked pepper
2	cups madeira sauce
1	teaspoon worcestershire sauce
2	tablespoons diable sauce
1 1/2	teaspoon dijon mustard
1	tablespoon red wine
2	tablespoons brandy

Place butter in skillet, when melted, add shallots and mushrooms. When shallots are slightly brown, add pepper, madeira sauce, worcestershire, diable sauce, dijon and wine. Mix well. Turn flame low and simmer for 10 minutes. Steak should be cooked to taste in a separate skillet. Pour brandy over meat. Heat on high flame, when very hot, ignite brandy. Dip steak in sauce and onto plates. Serve sauce on the side. Serves two.

WATERCOLORS

Dana Point Resort
25135 Park Lantern
Dana Point, CA
661-5000

Veal Loin with Buffalo Mozzarella and Shiitakes

2	3 1/2 ounce veal medallions, pounded thin
6	shiitake mushrooms, thinly sliced
3	basil leaves, coarsely chopped
3	ounces buffalo mozzarella, softened with cream
1	finely chopped shallot
1	ounce olive oil
	salt and pepper to taste

Mix the mozzarella with cream and basil to make a thick paste. In smoking hot olive oil, saute the mushrooms and shallots. Cook fast for 1 minute and remove from heat to cool. Spread the mozzarella mix over the medallions and place a handful of mushrooms in the center of each medallion. Fold the sides, roll up and skewer. In hot oil, brown both sides of the medallions and finish in an oven at 350 degrees for 8 to 10 minutes. Serve with the following sauce. Serves two.

Sauce:

1	garlic clove, diced
1	shallot, coarsely chopped
	shiitake mushroom stems, diced
4	ounces madeira wine
6	ounces demi glaze (reduced veal stock)
1	tablespoon sweet butter

In a hot saucepan, combine the garlic, shallots, stems and wine. Reduce by half. Add demi glaze and reduce by half again. Swirl in the butter, salt and pepper to taste. Serve over the veal rolls.

SALERNO RESTAURANT

220 Beach St.
Laguna Beach, CA
497-2600

Opened in 1975, this quaint little restaurant is one of the older standing businesses in Laguna Beach. The atmosphere is cozy with red and white checkered tablecloths. The faire is definitely Italian with a New York slant. Salerno is open daily for lunch and dinner.

Veal Parmigiana

1	pound veal, pounded into thin slices
2	beaten eggs
	bread crumbs
1/2	cup olive oil
1/2	cup vegetable oil
	tomato sauce, enough to cover bottom of pan and veal
1/2	pound sliced mozzarella

Dip the veal into the beaten eggs and cover with bread crumbs. Fry quickly in hot olive and vegetable oils. Remove the veal and place on paper towels to absorb excess oil. Pour off the leftover oil and discard. In the same pan, cover the bottom with tomato sauce. Add the veal and cover with the remaining sauce. Place the cheese over each serving. Put the pan in the oven just long enough to melt the cheese. Serve on heated plates. Serves four.

Veal Picatta

olive oil and corn oil
2 1/2   *pounds white provino veal, sliced paper thin*
4   *teaspoons marsala wine*
4   *teaspoons lemon juice*
8   *thin slices lemon*
8   *tablespoons water*
2   *teaspoons flour*
8   *ounces sliced mushrooms*
4   *teaspoons butter*

Heat half olive oil and half corn oil in a frying pan. Quickly fry the veal strips on each side. Pour off the excess oil, add the wine and lemon juice, lemon slices and water. Reduce. Dredge the veal in flour. Add to the wine mixture. Add mushrooms and butter. Heat for 5 minutes more. Serve on a large oval platter. Garnish with lemon slices. Serves four.

NOTES

ENTREES POULTRY

RISTORANTE FERRANTELLI

25001 Dana Point Harbor Dr.
Dana Point, CA
493-1401

Braciole di Pollo
(Chicken with Fresh Tomato Sauce)

4	chicken breasts, boneless and pounded flat
2	diced garlic cloves
2	ounces prosciutto
1	bunch parsley, coarsely chopped
1	ounce pine nuts, crushed
2	ounces grated parmesan cheese

Combine garlic, prosciutto, parsley, nuts and parmesan. Fill each breast with the mixture and roll up the breasts. Secure each roll with toothpicks. Top with tomato sauce and bake at 350 degrees until the breasts are golden brown. Garnish with parmesan cheese. Serves four.

Tomato sauce:

4	large tomatoes, steamed, peeled and diced
1	diced garlic clove
4	tablespoons olive oil
	pinch of rosemary

Slowly saute the tomatoes, garlic and rosemary in the olive oil for 15 to 20 minutes.

LA CAVE

1695 Irvine Ave.
Costa Mesa, CA
646-7944

Owner Carol Boyer must be doing something right. La Cave has been in operation for well over 30 years and continues to be a favorite today. This popular restaurant features top quality steaks and seafood. La Cave is open daily for lunch and dinner.

Breast of Chicken Acapulco

6	5 ounce pieces boneless chicken breasts
	bread crumbs
3	Ortega peppers
1	thinly sliced tomato
8	ounces King crab
1	sliced avocado
6	asparagus spears
9	ounces jack cheese
4	tablespoons parmesan cheese
12	ounces spanish sauce

Lightly bread the breasts and fry in cooking oil until golden brown. Place the breasts on paper towels to absorb any excess oil. Place the breasts on a cookie sheet. Cut the peppers in half lengthwise and place a piece on each of the breasts. Layer each breast with the tomato slices. Then staircase 1 piece of crab and 1 slice each avocado and asparagus spear. Top with jack cheese and parmesan. Pour spanish sauce into a shallow baking pan and place each breast in the sauce. Bake at 400 degrees until the cheeses melt. Serve with spanish rice. Serves six.

MARRAKESH

1100 W. Coast Hwy.
Newport Beach, CA
645-8384

B'Stila

1	*2 pound chicken*
2	*cups chopped onions*
1	*cup chopped parsley*
1	*pinch saffron*
1/2	*cup sweet butter*
1/2	*pint water*
	salt and pepper to taste
1/2	*cup powdered sugar*
5	*eggs*
2	*cups roasted ground almonds*
	sugar to taste (approximately 1/2 cup)
1	*tablespoon cinnamon*
4	*layers phyllo dough*

In a pot, combine chicken, onions, parsley, saffron, butter, water, salt and pepper. Bring to a boil then simmer on a low flame for about 45 minutes. When chicken is cooked, remove from pot and let cool. Scramble 5 eggs and add to the broth of chicken and cook for 12-15 minutes. Bone chicken and cut into small pieces. Mix almonds with sugar and cinnamon.

Brush a 12 inch diameter ovenproof frying pan or heavy casserole with melted butter. Lay phyllo dough in pan, making sure that about 5 inches of the dough hangs over the pan. In the following order, put a layer of almonds, a layer of chicken, a layer of almonds and a layer of eggs. Repeat until pan is full. Fold the outside phyllo dough to center of pan and bake for 15 minutes in 400 degree oven.

To serve, put B'Stila upside down on a nice platter. Top with powdered sugar and use a paper doily to make a decorative design with additional cinnamon. Serve hot. Serves six.

BENIHANA
4250 Birch St.
Newport Beach, CA
955-0822

Chicken with Benihana Magic Mustard Sauce

6	*ounces chicken breast, skinned, boned and diced*
1	*teaspoon soybean oil*
	salt and pepper to taste
1/2	*teaspoon sesame seeds*
1	*teaspoon lemon juice*

Heat a non-stick skillet. If using an electric skillet, set at 350 degrees. Add oil to the heated skillet. Season the chicken and cook 5 to 8 minutes or until the pieces are white and firm to the touch. Sprinkle with lemon juice and sesame seeds. Cook 2 to 3 minutes more and serve hot. Dip chicken in the mustard sauce. Serves one.

Benihana Magic Mustard Sauce:

3	*tablespoons dry mustard*
2	*tablespoons hot water*
1/2	*cup soy sauce*
2	*tablespoons sesame seeds, toasted*
1	*garlic clove, crushed*

In a small bowl, combine the mustard and water to make a paste. Transfer to a blender and add the remaining ingredients. Puree until smooth. Makes 6 servings or 2 tablespoons per serving. This may be used as a dressing for beans or alfalfa sprouts.

McCormick & Schmick's Seafood Restaurant
2000 Main St.
Irvine, CA
756-0505

Chicken Breast with Mango-Orange Barbecue Glaze

8   *3 ounce chicken breasts*
      oil to coat chicken

Mango-orange barbecue glaze:

1   *cup mango chutney (Major Grey's brand)*
1   *cup orange juice*
1/2   *cup barbecue sauce*

Combine the 3 ingredients in a blender and puree until smooth. Grill the breasts over a medium high fire 2 to 3 minutes per side. Baste frequently with the glaze. Glaze the top of the breasts with extra sauce as they come off the fire. Serves eight.

PARK AVENUE CAFE

501 Park Ave.
Balboa Island, CA
673-3830

Park Avenue Cafe is located one block from the Ferry Landing. For the past eight years, it has featured "casual fine dining." This cozy restaurant provides a lovely decor of floral tablecloths and crystal lamps. Denise Nicks has come up with a wonderful menu worthy of your attention. Sesame chicken, prime rib with yorkshire pudding and an English breakfast with bangers are just a few of the menu items. Moderately priced, Park Avenue Cafe is perhaps the best deal on Balboa Island.

Chicken Cordon Bleu

1	8 ounce chicken breast, boneless, skinless, cut in two
2	thin slices of ham
2	thin slices of swiss cheese
	bread crumbs
1	egg
	clarified butter

On each half breast, place ham and swiss cheese, roll up from end and hold together by inserting toothpick. Beat egg, roll prepared breasts in egg and bread crumbs. Saute in clarified butter until golden brown and place in hot oven for 10 minutes, or until chicken is tender. Place on plate and pour veloute sauce over each breast, serve with wild rice and steamed vegetables. Serves one.

Veloute Sauce:

2	ounces clarified butter
2	ounces flour
2	ounces heavy cream
1	cup hot chicken stock, seasoned and strained

Cook butter and flour for 1 minute, stirring constantly. Do not brown. Gradually add chicken stock to the roux (flour and butter). Stir with wire whisk until smooth. Check seasoning to taste, add two ounces heavy cream and cook until reduced to gravy thickness.

114

THE CANNERY

3010 Lafayette Ave.
Newport Beach, CA
675-5777

The Cannery is an important historical landmark in Newport. As the name implies, from 1921 to the early 1970's it was a fish cannery. However, as the local fishing industry declined, so did the cannery. In 1973, the Cannery was given new life and opened as a restaurant. Located on the waterfront in the historic Cannery Village, it has retained the old fish canning ambiance to compliment its award winning seafood dishes. The restaurant is locally owned and has been operated by the same group since its inception. They remain dedicated to the three pillars of all successful restaurants; great food, good service and interesting atmosphere. The Cannery is open daily for lunch, dinner and brunch on Sunday.

Chicken Champignon

1	8 ounce chicken breast, skinless
	flour to dust chicken
	salt and pepper to taste
3	canned artichoke hearts
1	tablespoon oil
3	large mushrooms, sliced
2	tablespoons butter
2	tablespoons lemon juice

Dredge breast in flour, season with salt and pepper. Saute chicken in heavy skillet with oil and 1 tablespoon butter over medium heat until golden brown on each side. Add 1 tablespoon butter, sliced mushrooms, lemon juice and artichoke hearts cut in half. Cover skillet and simmer about 20 minutes. Serves one.

NEWPORT LANDING

503 E. Edgewater
Balboa, CA
675-2373

Chicken with Lemon-Dijon Sauce

6   *8 ounce chicken breasts, grilled*

Lemon-Dijon sauce:

1   *quart chicken stock*
3   *tablespoons lemon juice*
1   *teaspoon granulated garlic*
1/2   *teaspoon each salt and pepper*
1/2   *teaspoon celery salt*
1   *teaspoon worcestershire sauce*
1 1/2 *cups dijon mustard*
1   *pint heavy cream*
2   *tablespoons white wine vinegar*
3   *tablespoons fresh dill, chopped*

Combine chicken stock, lemon juice, spices and worcestershire sauce. Over medium heat, reduce by half. Add mustard and cream and bring to a boil. Thicken with a butter and flour roux, then add vinegar and dill. Serve over chicken breasts. Serves six.

MARRAKESH

1100 W. Coast Hwy.
Newport Beach, CA
645-8384

Chicken with Lemon and Olives

1   *2 1/2 pound chicken*
1/2   *cup olive oil*
2   *onions, finely chopped*
1/2   *teaspoon chopped garlic*
       pinch of saffron
1/2   *teaspoon ginger*
       salt and pepper to taste
1   *can green olives, Graber brand*

1/2   quart water
rinds of 2 pickled lemons (See Note) or 2 fresh lemons

Brown chicken in olive oil; add onions, garlic and spices and simmer for 15 minutes on low heat. If using fresh lemons, add lemon rinds and water, cover and cook 45 minutes. Remove chicken from pot. Add olives and if using pickled lemons add lemon rinds and allow the sauce to thicken for 10 minutes. Serve chicken on a big platter topped with lemon rinds, olives and the sauce.

Note: To pickle lemons, slice each lemon lengthwise in 4 equal slices but do not slice entirely through. Fill lemons with salt, put in jar, cover with water and keep tightly closed for 3 weeks. Before using, rinse and then cook in boiling water for 3 minutes.

PARADISE CAFE

600 Newport Center Dr.
Newport Beach, CA
644-1237

Paradise Cafe's decor of oak floors, a carved oak Victorian bar, bentwood chairs and oak tables is the epitome of a San Francisco cafe. One gets the feeling of being in an atrium or greenhouse. The menu is varied and eclectic, offering a variety of choices. Reasonably priced and casual, one can kick back and not feel hurried. The Paradise Cafe is open daily for lunch and dinner. Closed Sundays.

Chicken Moutard

1   10 ounce chicken breast, skinned
1 1/4 ounces sweet butter
1   tablespoon peanut oil
*   flour*
2   mushrooms, quartered
3   ounces heavy cream
1   teaspoon whole grain mustard
1/4   teaspoon dijon mustard
1/8   teaspoon worcestershire sauce
*   salt and pepper to taste*

In an 8 inch skillet, melt 1/4 ounce of butter. Add oil and heat over a high flame. Lightly dust chicken breast in flour (shaking off excess) and brown in hot oil. Add mushrooms, cream, both mustards and worcestershire sauce. Place in a 400 degree oven for 6-8 minutes, or until done. Remove chicken from sauce and keep warm. Continue

cooking sauce on high heat until it thickens.   Remove from heat and let cool. Stir in remaining butter until melted. Add salt and pepper to taste. Spoon sauce over chicken and serve. Serves one.

GEN KAI JAPANESE RESTAURANT

3344 E. Coast Hwy.
Corona del Mar, CA
675-0771

Chicken Teriyaki, Ginger Flavor

1	*7 ounce chicken breast*
3 1/2	*tablespoons soy sauce*
2	*tablespoons sake*
1	*tablespoon sugar*
2	*teaspoons grated ginger*
1/2	*teaspoon oil*
1	*tablespoon chopped green onion*

Combine soy sauce, sake, sugar and grated ginger. Marinate chicken in sauce for 30 minutes. Brown both sides of chicken in oil in a small skillet over high heat. Reduce heat, cook until tender and serve on a warm plate. In the same skillet, boil down sauce a little, and serve over chicken. Garnish with chopped green onion. Makes one serving.

RUMPELSTILTSKIN'S

114 McFadden Pl.
Newport Beach, CA
673-5025

Lemon-Herb Chicken

4	*boneless chicken breasts*

Lemon-Herb marinade:

1	*cup lemon juice*
1	*cup safflower oil*
1/4	*cup minced garlic*
3/4	*cup chopped Italian parsley*
1	*tablespoon minced fresh tarragon*

1/2	teaspoon lemon pepper
1/2	teaspoon minced fresh oregano
1/2	teaspoon minced fresh thyme
1/2	teaspoon ground cumin
1	tablespoon sugar

Combine all marinade ingredients and marinate chicken breasts in refrigerator for 4 hours. On a hot grill, place the breasts skin side down. The oil in the marinade will cause the grill to flame up, so keep a squirt bottle handy. Sear the skin well before turning. Cook 3 minutes. Remove the skin with tongs and a knife. Baste the breasts and turn over to finish. Serve with rice pilaf and a favorite steamed vegetable.

THE PALM GARDEN

Sheraton Newport Beach Hotel
4545 MacArthur Blvd.
Newport Beach, CA
833-0570

The Palm Garden, located in the Sheraton Hotel across from John Wayne Airport offers fine dining with a charming Mediterranean decor. The menu offers the combination of Italian and California cuisine. Chef Lewis Friedman offers this delectable chicken recipe to whet your appetite.

Mesquite Grilled Chicken Breast Stuffed with Goat Cheese and Sun Dried Tomatoes with Roasted Garlic Rosemary Butter

| 4 | 8 ounce chicken breasts, skin on |

Goat Cheese and Sun Dried Tomatoes Stuffing:

6	ounces goat cheese
2	ounces cream cheese
1	tablespoon chopped garlic
2	tablespoons sun dried tomatoes

Whip the ingredients together in a mixer for about 5 minutes until smooth. Place about 2 ounces of the stuffing under the skin of the breasts. Brush with olive oil and salt and ground pepper to taste. Place the breasts on the mesquite grill, meat side down. After a few minutes, remove and place in a 450 degree oven until golden brown. Once fully cooked, baste with the softened roasted garlic rosemary butter. Serves four.

Roasted Garlic Rosemary Butter:

60	*garlic cloves*
1/2	*cup chopped fresh rosemary*
1	*pound butter*
1	*tablespoon salt*
2	*teaspoons cracked black pepper*
	juice of 3 lemons

Place the garlic in a pan with a little olive oil. Roast at 375 degrees in the oven until golden brown. Once cool, finely chop the garlic and place in mixing bowl. Add the remaining ingredients and whip until smooth.

SPLASHES
Surf & Sand Hotel
1555 S. Coast Hwy.
Laguna Beach, CA
497-4477

Splashes is appealingly "beachy" with glass balustrades affording an uninterrupted ocean view through open French windows. Although the menu is inspired by a rich variety of food products and dishes from Mediterranean countries including Morocco, Spain, southern France, Italy and Greece, it is, nevertheless uniquely its own creative statement. It is the spirit and experience of California cuisine which has made it all come together. There is a sophisticated informality about the food and the setting which fulfills one's expectations of oceanfront dining in the heart of California's Riviera.

Moroccan Spiced Chicken in Phyllo Dough

4	*chicken breasts, grilled and diced*
2	*diced onions*
1/2	*teaspoon coriander*
1/2	*teaspoon tumeric*
1/2	*teaspoon cinnamon*
1/2	*teaspoon cumin*
	salt and pepper to taste
1/2	*teaspoon saffron*
4	*cups chicken stock*
12	*sheets phyllo dough*
1/2	*cup melted butter*
3/4	*cup mint*
1	*cup raisins*
1	*cup almonds*

120

Grill chicken and dice and set aside. Saute the onions in butter until translucent. Add the seasonings, raisins, almonds and saute for 5 to 10 minutes. Add the chicken stock and reduce until the stock is dissolved. Add the chicken to the mixture and set aside.

Carefully lay 1 sheet of phyllo dough on a flat surface and lightly baste with melted butter. Gently lay a second sheet on top and lightly smooth out any wrinkles. Repeat the first step 1 more time. When the mixture is cool, spoon 5 to 6 ounces onto the dough. Roll into 1 inch diameter rolls. Press the ends tight so the filling will not come out when baking. Bake at 400 degrees for 15 minutes. Serves four.

MULDOON'S IRISH PUB & RESTAURANT

202 Newport Center Dr.
Newport Beach, CA
640-4110

Muldoon's decor is reminiscent of a typical pub one might find in Dublin. Dark wood and brass trim the pub and offer a quiet ambiance. For over 18 years, Muldoon's has had a menu featuring Irish manor house foods, as well as burgers, salads, wonderfully grilled fresh fish and freshly baked Irish soda bread. Muldoon's is open daily for lunch and dinner. Sunday brunch is also served.

Old Bushmill's Chicken

3	ounces virgin olive oil
2	fresh garlic cloves, crushed
4	6 ounce boneless chicken breasts, skin removed and washed
1/2	ounce Old Bushmill's Irish Whiskey
1/2	ounce white wine
1/4	ounce red sweet pepper, sliced thin
1/4	ounce green scallions, chopped
2	medium carrots, chopped and steamed soft
4	ounces frozen petite peas
4	ounces fresh broccoli, sliced on diagonal and steamed
1	bunch fresh spinach, washed and drained
1	8 ounce package of wild rice, cooked per directions on package
	salt and pepper to taste

Sauce:

3	ounces dijon mustard
4	ounces half and half
2	ounces honey

121

In a large skillet, put 2-3 ounces olive oil; when hot, add garlic. Allow it to simmer but not brown. Turn heat to medium, add pepper and chicken breasts. Saute until the meat turns white on both sides, do not overcook. Add the whiskey and white wine, simmer 1 minute until it bubbles. Take off flame and reserve to the side.

In another heavy skillet, saute red pepper, green scallions and spinach with 1 ounce olive oil for 30 seconds. Now spoon in 1/2 of the reserved whiskey liquid over the vegetables and simmer for 30 seconds until all are soft but still vibrant in color. Add the chicken to this mixture and lower heat. In the empty skillet, saute the carrots, peas and broccoli with the remaining liquid. Combine the mustard, half and half and honey over low heat. Serve on the side.

On a large platter, top the hot wild rice with the chicken breasts, spinach, other cooked vegetables and sauce. Garnish with a sprig of cilantro.

ROYAL THAI CUISINE
4001 W. Coast Hwy.
Newport Beach, CA
645-8424

Patpong Chicken

2	cups chicken meat, cut up
1	tablespoon Maggi sauce
4	tablespoons oyster sauce
1/4	cup oil
1	tablespoon dried chilies, without seeds
2	garlic cloves, crushed
3-4	large shrimp
1	tablespoon fish sauce
2	pinches white pepper
1	cup raw cashew nuts, unsalted

Marinate chicken in combined Maggi and oyster sauces for 1 hour. Heat oil in a wok, stir fry chilies and brown garlic. Add chicken, then shrimp with the fish sauce and remaining marinade. Cook until done (3-5 minutes), then add cashews and stir fry 3 seconds.

STUFT NOODLE
215 Riverside Ave.
Newport Beach, CA
646-2333

Pollo Arrabiata
(Chicken Breast in Spicy Marinara)

2	ounces olive oil
4	pieces chicken breasts
	flour
	pinch black pepper
1	tablespoon garlic
2	scallions, minced
	pinch hot red pepper
1/2	pound mushrooms, sliced
1/2	cup white wine
8	ounces pear tomatoes in juice and chopped
4	leaves fresh basil, minced

Heat olive oil in a skillet. Roll breasts in flour and season with black pepper. Saute breasts in oil 4 minutes. Put breasts to the side and remove excess oil. Add garlic, scallion, red pepper and mushroom and saute for 1 minute. Return chicken to the pan. Add wine, tomatoes and basil and simmer on high heat 3-4 minutes or until sauce is smooth. Serves four.

ANTONELLO RISTORANTE
South Coast Plaza Village
1611 W. Sunflower Ave.
Santa Ana, CA
751-7153

Pollo Cinque Erbe
(Chicken in Five Herbs Sauce)

1   *skinless chicken breast, pounded, grilled or seared in hot olive oil*

Five Herb Sauce:

1   *tablespoon fresh basil, chopped*
1   *tablespoon fresh Italian parsley, chopped*
1   *teaspoon dried oregano*
1   *teaspoon fresh rosemary, chopped*
2   *teaspoons chopped chives*
1   *minced garlic clove*
1   *teaspoon crushed red chili*
1   *cup extra virgin olive oil*
       salt and pepper to taste

Combine all the ingredients in a mixing bowl. Ladle over the grilled breasts. Serves one.

This sauce is excellent with grilled fish such as swordfish, salmon, sea bass, halibut or orange roughy as well.

ROTHCHILD'S RESTAURANT

2407 E. Coast Hwy.
Corona del Mar, CA
673-3750

Rothchild's is a quaint, intimate restaurant featuring fine Northern Italian cuisine. Their specialties include homemade pastas and fresh seafood dishes. They also feature a large selection of domestic and imported wines. Lunch is served Monday through Friday and dinner is served nightly. Be sure to take time to enjoy the beautiful art collection throughout the restaurant.

Pollo Orangeo
(Chicken Breasts with Fresh Orange Sauce)

4-6 chicken breasts, lightly breaded and grilled, keep warm in oven

Fresh orange sauce:

1/4	cup olive oil
1	tablespoon chopped garlic
3	cups fresh orange juice
	juice from 2 lemons
2	tablespoons brown sugar
4	teaspoons orange blossom honey
1/2	cup cooking sherry
1	tablespoon cornstarch
1	large orange, peeled and wedged
4	ounces whipped butter

Saute garlic in olive oil. Add orange juice, lemon juice, brown sugar and honey. Bring to a boil, add sherry, cornstarch, orange wedges and butter. Simmer for 3 minutes. Serve over chicken breasts. Variation: Substitute orange wedges with pineapple, raspberry, or a mixture of all three.

ANTOINE

Le Meridien Hotel
4500 MacArthur Blvd.
Newport Beach, CA
476-2001

Roasted Quail with a Mushroom Rizotto
and Black Currant Sauce

8	quail, boned
1	pound fresh spinach, stemmed, washed and dried
4	ounces bacon or ham
3	ounces rizotto rice or basmati rice, washed
1/2	pound shiitake mushrooms, washed, dried and diced
6	shallots, peeled and coarsely chopped
1	pint chicken stock
1	bunch chives, coarsely chopped
1	bunch thyme, coarsely chopped

Cut the bacon into fine julienne and saute in a hot pan until very crispy. Drain well, return to heat and add the spinach leaves. Saute until the leaves are soft. Salt and pepper to taste. Remove from heat, drain and set aside to cool. Season the quail inside and out. Stuff each bird with the bacon and spinach. Reserve in the refrigerator. Saute the shiitakes in a little butter until soft. Drain well. Saute the shallots until soft in the remaining butter. Add the mushrooms and rice. Mix well. Cover with chicken stock and gently simmer. Stir continually and if necessary, add more chicken stock until the rice is thoroughly cooked. Mix in the chopped herbs and check seasoning. Keep hot.

Roast the quail in a hot oven at 400 degrees for 5 to 7 minutes until golden brown. Drain off excess juices.

Black Currant sauce:

1	small onion, chopped
1	cup red wine
1	4 ounce jar black currants in syrup
1	pint veal stock

Saute the onion in a little oil until light brown. Add the wine and reduce until almost a glaze. Add most of the black currants and syrup. Reserve 2 tablespoons for garnish. Cook for 2 to 3 minutes. Add the veal stock and simmer for 20 minutes continually skimming the sauce. Pass through a fine strainer and check seasonings. Keep hot.

126

For presentation, place 2 quail on a plate. Press the rizotto in a round mold (5 cm. x 4 cm.) above the quail at the top of the plate. Stir the remaining black currants into the sauce. Bring to a boil and spoon over the quail. Garnish with fresh herbs. Serves four.

SHANGHAI PINE GARDENS

300 Marine Ave.
Balboa Island, CA
673-3802

Sauteed Chicken and Shrimp

1/4	pound white chicken meat, sliced
1/4	pound shrimp, 41-50 size, peeled and veined

Dredge for chicken and shrimp:

> salt to taste
> tapioca flour
> egg white

2	tablespoons oil
7	flowers broccoli
7	snow peas
2	pieces carrot, slices
1	garlic clove, minced
1/2	teaspoon sugar
3/4	cup chicken broth

Dredge chicken and shrimp. In 2 tablespoons of oil, fry the chicken and shrimp in a wok for less than a minute. Add the vegetables and cook for about 20 seconds. Add garlic, salt to taste, sugar and broth and stir fry for another 20-30 seconds. Serve with steamed rice. Serves two.

THE QUIET WOMAN
3224 E. Coast Hwy.
Corona del Mar, CA
640-7440

Teriyaki Chicken

4   10 ounce boneless chicken breasts

Teriyaki marinade and glaze:

2   cups soy sauce
1   cup cooking sherry
2 3/4   cups water
1/2   pound brown sugar
1 1/2   teaspoons ground ginger
*   cornstarch to thicken*

Combine the five marinade ingredients in a saucepan and bring to boil. Boil for 15 minutes. Pour off 2/3 for marinade. Mix cornstarch with water to make a paste, add to remainder and simmer until thick, set aside. Marinate chicken overnight. Remove from marinade and discard marinade. Brush breasts with thickened teriyaki glaze and charbroil until done, basting as needed. Serves four.

TREES
440 Heliotrope Ave.
Corona del Mar, CA
673-0910

Thai Fried Chicken

2 1/2   pounds boneless chicken, cut into pieces 1/2 x 2-3 inches
1 1/2   cups snow peas
1   cup matchstick cut carrots
1   cup matchstick cut leeks
1   cup matchstick cut jicama or daikon
1/2   cup julienne red peppers
1/2   cup julienne gold peppers
1/2   cup julienne green peppers
2-4   teaspoons "Sambal Olec" (hot chili paste)
1/2   cup beef or chicken stock
3   cups steamed sweet rice

Marinade for chicken:

1	cup soya sauce
1	cup roasted sesame oil
2	tablespoons minced garlic
2	tablespoons ground coriander
1	tablespoon sugar
1	tablespoon black pepper
1/4	cup coarsely chopped cilantro
1/4	cup coarsely chopped green onion

Prepare the marinade by combining all ingredients and mixing well. Place the chicken in a bowl and cover with enough marinade so it is well covered and coated but not swimming in it. Cut all the vegetables and lay them out in separate piles. Cook the sweet rice and hold it over steam to keep it warm. Preheat a thin skillet to smoking hot and add 1 ounce peanut oil. Add the chicken to the skillet and let it cook until well browned on one side. Toss chicken to brown the other side (7-10 minutes). Toss the vegetables over the chicken and stir while frying until they are combined but still crisp. Add the Sambal Olec. Quickly add the stock and toss for 15 seconds. Arrange on a plate and top with a serving of the sweet rice. Serves six.

NOTES

ENTREES SEAFOOD

WOODY'S WHARF

2318 Newport Blvd.
Newport Beach, CA
675-0474

Abalone

6	*ounces abalone, pounded flat*
2	*tablespoons flour*
1	*whole egg*
2	*tablespoons butter*
2	*tablespoons white wine*
2	*tablespoons lemon juice*

Pound abalone until flat. Do not be afraid to pound well. Combine flour and egg, dip abalone and saute in butter. Add wine and lemon juice. Cook about 1 minute on each side. Do not overcook as the abalone will lose its tenderness. Serve with rice pilaf. Serves one.

AMELIA'S

311 Marine Ave.
Balboa Island, CA
673-6580

Located on the main street of Balboa Island for over 30 years, Amelia's has been serving the residents and visitors of Newport who cherish the finest in delectable pasta and exquisite seafood. This quaint European style restaurant offers lunch during the week and dinner every evening. Brunch is served on Sunday.

Amelia's Lady Sole

1	whole egg
1 1/2	cup fine bread crumbs
1	cup milk
12	small sole filets
18	scallops, chopped
3/4	cup butter
1/2	cup flour
1	cup mushrooms, sliced and sauteed
1	cup Alaskan king crab, cooked
	salt and pepper
1	cup cheddar cheese, grated
1	cup semi-dry sherry
1	tablespoon chopped parsley
1	tablespoon chopped chives
4	tablespoons almonds, toasted and sliced

Beat the egg and combine with milk, dip filets in mixture and then in the bread crumbs. Arrange scallops on only 6 of the filets, brush with butter. Broil the filets for 5 minutes or bake at 350 degrees for 12 minutes. Place plain filets on top of the others. In a separate pan, melt remaining butter and combine with flour to make a smooth paste. Add mushrooms, crab, salt and pepper to taste. Stir in cheddar cheese, chives, parsley and sherry. Cook into a smooth sauce by adding remaining egg and milk mixture. Do not boil. Pour sauce over the layered sole. Garnish with the almonds. Serves six.

TETE A TETE
217 Marine Ave.
Balboa Island, CA
673-0570

Atlantic Salmon Filet with Cucumber and Dill Sauce

4   *7 ounce Atlantic Salmon filets, skin off*

Salt and pepper to taste and brush with olive oil. Saute in a hot skillet or grill for 4 to 6 minutes on each side. Serve on top of the sauce. Garnish with dried tomatoes and a sprig of dill. Serves four.

Cucumber and Dill sauce:

1   *small finely chopped brown onion*
3   *cucumbers, peeled, seeded and sliced*
1/4   *cup Champagne wine vinegar*
1/2   *cup dry white wine*
2   *cups heavy whipping cream*
2   *tablespoons chopped dill*
        salt and white pepper to taste
2   *tablespoons olive oil*

Heat skillet with 1 tablespoon olive oil. Saute onions until soft but not brown. Add cucumber and deglaze with vinegar and wine. Reduce for 2 minutes and add whipping cream. Season to taste. Reduce more if desired. Shortly before serving add the chopped dill.

THE ALLEY

4501 W. Coast Hwy.
Newport Beach, CA
646-9126

Baked Halibut

1	8-10 ounce halibut steak
1/2	ounce butter
	pinch of garlic
2	ounces white wine
2	ounces diced tomatoes
1/2	teaspoon capers
2	ounces au jus
	parsley sprig
	twist of lemon rind

In a skillet, melt butter, then add garlic, wine, tomatoes, capers and au jus. Bring to a simmer and add halibut. Saute until brown. In a preheated oven, bake the halibut for 10 minutes at 400 degrees. Garnish with parsley and lemon rind.

McCORMICK & SCHMICK'S

2000 Main St.
Irvine, CA
756-0505

Baked Halibut with Crab and Brie*

1	cup beurre blanc sauce
4	5 ounce halibut filets, not steaks
6	ounces dungeness crab meat
6	ounces brie, cut into 1/2 inch cubes
1	tablespoon fresh dill, chopped
	pinch salt and pepper

Preheat oven to 400 degrees. Prepare the beurre blanc sauce and reserve. Split the filets lengthwise to form a pocket for the stuffing. Combine the crab, brie, dill and season. Divide the stuffing mixture between the 4 filets. When full, let the flaps cover the stuffing so that only a small amount is exposed. Bake in a lightly buttered baking dish for 10 to 12 minutes. Remove to dinner plates and spoon the sauce over the fish. Serves four.
*This recipe is a variation from "McCormick & Schmick's Seafood Cookbook".

Baked Ling Cod with Brie, Apples, Pine Nuts and Butter Sauce

1	ling cod filet
1	ounce brie cheese
1/2	ounce clarified butter
1/4	ounce apple slices
1/2	tablespoon pine nuts
1/2	teaspoon chopped parsley
1	ounce butter sauce

Make a pocket in the filet and stuff with the brie. Heat a saute pan, add butter and the filet. Saute until about 3/4 done. Finish the filet in the oven. Remove the filet from the pan and add the apples, pine nuts, parsley and butter sauce. Serves one.

Butter sauce:

2	tablespoons white wine vinegar
4	tablespoons white wine
2	tablespoons heavy cream
1	tablespoon chopped shallot
1/2	cup unsalted butter, cut into pieces

In a medium saucepan, add vinegar, wine and shallot. Reduce until almost evaporated. Add the cream and reduce until thickened. Remove from heat and stir in butter, a piece at a time until the sauce forms. Strain and set aside.

OYSTERS

2515 E. Coast Hwy.
Corona del Mar, CA
675-7411

Baked Salmon in Phyllo with Orange-Ginger Sauce

12   ounces salmon, skinned, boned
1/2   bunch fresh spinach, cleaned and stems removed
2   red peppers, roasted, seeded, peeled
1   package phyllo
2   cups fresh orange juice
3   teaspoons fresh ginger, chopped
3   cups heavy cream

Cut Salmon in 1/2 inch strips. Layout two sheets of phyllo dough on a cookie sheet. Layout spinach leaf in a 3 by 5 rectangle. Shingle salmon strips over the spinach and top with the red peppers. Fold bottom layer of phyllo over the spinach, salmon and red peppers. Fold over the ends, refold down the length resulting in a 3 by 5 rectangle. Make two of these. Bake in a 400 degree oven until golden brown. Slice lengthwise.

Orange-Ginger Sauce:

Heat the orange juice and ginger (soft boil) until thick and syrupy. In another pan, reduce the heavy cream by half. Add the orange juice and ginger and bring to a simmer. Hint: (Syrup reduction and sauce takes about 20 minutes. It is best to have the syrup done early and add to reduced cream about 10 minutes before the salmon is done.) Pour sauce over each half of salmon. Makes two servings.

BLUE BEET CAFE

107 21st Pl.
Newport Beach, CA
675-2338

Bay Scallops, Gina Marie

1 1/2 pounds bay scallops
1   cup chopped shallots
6   sweet basil leaves
5   tablespoons chopped green onions
3   tablespoons chopped parsley
8   ounces small mushrooms
4   garlic cloves, crushed
       salt and pepper to taste
1   ounce Pernod or Anisette
1   cup heavy cream

In a large pan, saute onions until transparent. Combine all the ingredients and bring to a simmer. Add bay scallops and cook for 2 minutes. Serve on a bed of angel hair pasta with fresh baked rolls and a steamed vegetable.

THE ARCHES
3334 W. Coast Hwy.
Newport Beach, CA
645-7077

Bouillabaisse Arches

1/8	cup olive oil
3/4	cup chopped onion
1	white part of leek, sliced thin
1	garlic clove, crushed
1	small carrot, sliced thin
3	medium tomatoes, peeled
2	sprigs parsley
4	cups water
1/4	teaspoon salt
4	crab legs
8	large shrimp
12	ounces swordfish, cut to bite size pieces
12	ounces halibut, cut to bite size pieces
12	mussels
12	clams
8	ounces lobster
1/4	teaspoon white pepper
1/8	teaspoon saffron, crumbled
1	cup white wine

In a large kettle, cook onions, leeks and garlic in hot oil until onions are transparent. Add carrots, parsley, tomatoes, salt, fish, shellfish and water. Cover and bring to boiling point. Reduce heat and simmer 15 minutes. Add saffron, pepper and wine. Simmer for 8-10 minutes more. Makes 4 large servings.

THE WINE CELLAR

Hyatt Newporter
1107 Jamboree Rd.
Newport Beach, CA
729-1234

Braise de Blanc d'Espadon en Ecaille de Courgettes
(Braised Swordfish in Zucchini Scale)

4	6 ounce swordfish steaks
2	green zucchini, sliced thin
2	yellow zucchini, sliced thin
	butter
1	ounce shallots, chopped
6	ounces fish stock

Cut slices of green and yellow zucchini in half. Top the fish steaks with the slices of zucchini, alternating colors to resemble fish scales. In a large pan, place the shallots on butter, and place the fish on top of the shallots. Add fish stock, making sure the stock does not cover the steaks. Cover pan and bake in 350 degree oven 10-15 minutes, or until fish is cooked through. Remove from pan and serve on a bed of Ratatouille au Coriander. See Potpourri section for this recipe.

FIVE CROWNS

3801 E. Coast Hwy.
Corona del Mar, CA
760-0331

Broiled Salmon with Dill Caper Sauce

4	8 ounce salmon filets
1	tablespoon olive oil
2	cups sour cream
1/4	cup mayonnaise
1/4	cup catsup
1	tablespoon prepared horseradish
1	tablespoon dijon mustard
1/3	cup capers, drained
1/4	cup chopped fresh dill

Brush salmon filets with olive oil. Broil about 4 minutes on each side. Combine remaining ingredients to make the sauce. Top the salmon filets with sauce. Serves four.

JOHN DOMINIS
2901 W. Coast Hwy.
Newport Beach, CA
650-5112

Cioppino

Aromatic Cilantro-white wine base:

3/4	cup olive oil
2	medium onions, sliced thin
2	large leeks, cleaned and sliced thin
3	garlic cloves, chopped
1/4	teaspoon finely chopped fresh jalapeno pepper
1	tablespoon chopped fresh fennel
4	quarts fish stock
2	quarts bottled clam juice
1	cup dry white wine
1	sprig fresh thyme, chopped fine
1/4	bunch fresh cilantro, chopped fine
4	bay leaves
	pinch saffron

Seafood:

1/2	pound scallops
1/2	pound lobster meat
18	clams, scrubbed
12	New Zealand green lip mussels or others, scrubbed
12	ounces shrimp, in shell
12	ounces king crab legs
1	pound sea bass filets or Pacific snapper

Finishing:

3	large tomatoes, peeled and coarsely chopped
	salt and pepper to taste

Bring olive oil to a slow simmer in heavy saucepan. Add onions, leeks, garlic, jalapeno and fennel and simmer until onions are transparent with slightly brown edges. In another large, wide saucepan combine fish stock, clam juice and wine. Cook over medium heat until 1/3 of liquid remains. Add reduced liquid to onion mixture. Add thyme, cilantro, bay leaves and saffron and simmer 10 minutes. Bring soup base to a simmer and add scallop, lobster, clams and mussels and simmer 5 minutes. Add shrimp, king crab and sea bass and simmer 4-6 minutes or until clams and mussels are open and other seafood is tender. At serving time, stir in tomatoes and salt and pepper to taste. Serves six.

WATERCOLORS

Dana Point Resort
25135 Park Lantern
Dana Point, CA
661-5000

Dover Sole with Spinach Mousse and Macadamia Nuts

12	*Dover sole filets, slightly pounded*
6	*ounces macadamia nuts, coarsely chopped*

Spinach Mousse:

2	*bunches fresh spinach, cooked, cooled and drained well*
1	*whole egg*
4	*ounces heavy butter*
	salt, pepper and nutmeg to taste

In a food processor, blend spinach and in order, add the remaining ingredients. Blend until there is a smooth consistency. Refrigerate for 20 minutes. Layout the filets and spread the mousse evenly over the filets. Roll the filets jelly roll style beginning at the large end. Roll the outside of the fish rolls in the macadamia nuts. Place the rolls in a lightly greased baking dish and bake at 350 degrees for about 12 minutes. Make a mirror of the basil butter sauce on a plate and place cooked fish rolls on the plate. Garnish with peeled and halved plum tomatoes.

Basil Butter Sauce:

3   ounces white wine
2   finely chopped shallots
2   ounces white wine vinegar
6   ounces heavy cream
8   ounces butter, softened
1   bunch sweet basil, coarsely chopped

Combine the wine, shallots and vinegar. Reduce by 1/2 over low heat. Add cream and reduce again by 1/2. Whip in the butter and basil. Season to taste. Remove from heat.

JOHN DOMINIS

2901 W. Coast Hwy.
Newport Beach, CA
650-5112

Dragon and the Phoenix

8   ounces peanut oil
1 1/4   pounds large shrimp, peeled and veined
1 1/2   pounds chicken breasts, cubed
1   tablespoon finely diced shallots
1   tablespoon finely chopped garlic
3/4   cup dry white wine
12   ounces curry sauce (see recipe below)
6   ounces peanut oil
2 1/4   pounds egg linguini, cooked in boiling water until tender. Drain and put in ice water
         for 15 seconds, drain and hold.
1   ounce fresh lemon juice
1/4   bunch fresh mint, chopped fine
         salt and pepper to taste
6   ounces mango chutney (see recipe below or purchase at store)
6   stalks green onion, tops only, chopped

In a large skillet, saute shrimp and chicken in peanut oil until half way cooked. Drain off remaining oil. Add shallots and garlic and stir for 30 seconds with shrimp and chicken over medium heat. Add wine and reduce 3/4. Add curry sauce and mix in. Turn off heat and hold mixture in warm place.

In a large skillet, saute cooked pasta in peanut oil until hot, add lemon, mint and salt and pepper to taste. Arrange pasta on serving plates. Place shrimp and chicken mixture on top of each plate of pasta. Add about 1 ounce mango chutney in middle of dish, sprinkle with chopped green onions and serve immediately. Serves six.

Curry sauce:

2	ounces peanut oil
1	garlic clove, chopped fine
1/2	teaspoon finely chopped ginger
1/2	small Maui or other sweet onion, diced fine
2	tablespoons curry powder
1	banana, overripe and mashed
1	bay leaf
3/4	cup rice vinegar
1/2	cup miran wine (sweet Japanese rice wine)
1	quart fish stock
3/4	cup cream or half and half
1/2	cup guava jelly
1/2	lime, juice squeezed
1	dash cayenne pepper
	corn starch, diluted in water, as needed

In a medium skillet, saute garlic, ginger and sweet onion in peanut oil until transparent. Add curry powder, banana and bay leaf and continue to cook for 1 1/2 minutes. Add rice vinegar, miran wine and fish stock. Reduce by 3/4. Add cream, guava jelly, lime and cayenne pepper and bring to a boil. Thicken with diluted corn starch, until it reaches medium thickness. Pull from heat and hold.

Mango chutney:

1	cup rice vinegar
1 1/2	cups passion fruit puree or juice
1	green onion stalk, chopped fine
2	serrano chilies, cleaned of stems, seeds and ribs, chopped fine
1	tablespoon fresh ginger, chopped fine with juice
2	teaspoons chili powder
1	teaspoon curry powder
1	mango, ripe, peeled and diced medium
1	tablespoon finely chopped fresh basil and mint
1	red onion, diced fine

In a medium sauce pan, combine rice vinegar, passion fruit juice, green onions, chilies, ginger, chili powder and curry powder and reduce by 3/4. Remove from heat and strain into a bowl. Add mango, fresh mint, basil and red onion. Mix thoroughly, cover and refrigerate for about 2 hours before using.

CANO'S
2241 W. Coast Hwy.
Newport Beach, CA
631-1331

Located on the Newport Harbor, along Coast Highway, this unique restaurant offers not your traditional Mexican faire but one that is heavily weighted to the seafoods of Mexico. Lunch and dinner are offered daily with brunch on Sunday. Entertainment is also offered most evenings. Chef Javier Zambrano offers this popular dish for your pleasure.

Dungeness Crab Cakes with Dijon Mustard and Lime Sauce

8	ounces crab meat, back fin
1	egg
3	tablespoons mayonnaise
1/4	teaspoon worcestershire sauce
1	teaspoon dijon mustard
1/2	teaspoon tabasco
	salt and pepper to taste
1/2	cup bread crumbs

Blend the wet ingredients and then add the dry ingredients. Fold in the crabmeat and form into 2 ounce patties. Dip the patties in the bread crumbs for an even coating on both sides. Saute for about 1 minute and serve with the mustard lime sauce. Serves one.

Dijon Mustard and Lime Sauce:

2	cups heavy cream
6	teaspoons dijon mustard
	juice of 1 lime
	salt and pepper to taste

Over a low flame, bring the cream to a boil, reducing until the bubbles are glossy. Whisk the mustard and lime juice into the cream. Season to taste. Heat for 1 minute for a thick consistency.

PAVILION
Four Seasons Hotel
690 Newport Center Dr.
Newport Beach, CA
759-0808

Grilled Ahi with a Balsamic Herb Sauce

1	7 ounce ahi steak, at least 1 inch thick
1	package enokis
2	ounces shallot rings
2	ounces diced tomatoes
10	ounces chicken stock
1	tablespoon finely chopped tarragon
1	tablespoon finely chopped parsley
1	tablespoon finely chopped chives
1	tablespoon finely chopped thyme
1-2	ounces whole butter
	salt and pepper to taste

In a very hot pan with olive oil, saute the tuna medallions that have been seasoned with salt and pepper. Brown well on each side, leaving the middle medium rare. Remove the tuna from the pan and pour off the excess fat. Add the enokis, shallots and tomatoes, saute well. Deglaze with the vinegar. Reduce by a third. Add chicken stock and boil. Add all the herbs and simmer for 2 minutes. Whip in whole butter. Season and serve. Serves four.

McCORMICK & SCHMICK'S
2000 Main St.
Irvine, CA
756-0505

Grilled Mahi Mahi with Mango-Orange Barbecue Glaze*

4	mahi mahi filets, 4 to 6 ounces each
	oil to coat fish

Barbecue the filets over a medium high fire, 3 to 4 minutes per side, basting frequently with sauce, until the filets are just cooked through. Glaze the top of the filets with extra sauce as they come off the fire. Serves four.

Mango-Orange Barbecue Glaze:

1   *cup mango chutney (Major Grey's brand)*
1   *cup orange juice*
1/2   *cup barbecue sauce, homemade or commercial*

Combine all the ingredients in a blender and puree until the solids in the chutney are smooth.

*This is an original recipe from Executive Chef Joe Gonzales and reprinted from "McCormick & Schmick's Seafood Cookbook".

RENATO
2304 W. Oceanfront
Newport Beach, CA
673-8058

Halibut al Tarragon

4   *8 ounce fresh Alaskan halibut filets*

Grill the filets until almost done. Finish by cooking in the sauce. Serves four.

Sauce:

8   *tablespoons fish broth*
4   *tablespoons dry white wine*
2   *tablespoons chopped fresh tarragon*
2   *tablespoons heavy whipping cream*

Combine all the ingredients and saute over medium flame. Reduce to desired thickness.

THE WAREHOUSE
3450 Via Oporto
Newport Beach, CA
673-4700

Halibut Scallops Bercy

4   *7 ounces halibut filets*
12   *ounces bay scallops*
2   *ounces butter*
2   *cups Bercy sauce*

Bercy Sauce:

2   *tablespoons shallots, minced*
4   *tablespoons butter or margarine*
4   *tablespoons flour*
2   *cups clam broth*
     salt and pepper to taste

Heat butter in saucepan and saute shallots until softened. Do not brown. Blend in flour, salt and pepper. Heat and stir until bubbly. Gradually add the clam broth and whisk until blended and smooth. Bring to a boil and simmer 2-3 minutes longer. Reserve and keep warm.

Coat halibut filets in seasoned flour. Saute in butter on both sides. Cook slightly underdone to prevent it from becoming dry. Remove filets and place on a plate and cover with foil to keep warm.

Melt 2 ounces butter in a saucepan and saute scallops very quickly. (Caution: Do not overcook or they will become rubbery.) Add Bercy sauce and bring to a simmer quickly. Place filets on serving dishes and top each with the scallop sauce. Garnish with lemon and parsley. Serves four.

ANTOINE

Le Meridien Hotel, Newport Beach
4500 MacArthur Blvd.
Newport Beach, CA
476-2001

John Dory wrapped in Potato with Saffron Sauce

4	*4 ounce John Dory filets*
6	*large potatoes, peeled*
	clarified butter

Using a mandolin, fine slice the potatoes and season. Lay out the potato slices into a rectangular shape, slightly larger than the filet. Spoon some of the tomato stuffing onto the potato rectangle. Place the filet on top. Add 1 more spoonful of tomato and cover with a layer of potato slices. Shallow fry the filets in hot clarified butter until golden brown and crispy on both sides. To serve, slice the filets diagonally. Place the 2 halves in the center of the plate. Spoon the sauce around the filets. Garnish with fresh herbs. Serve immediately. Serves four.

Filling:

1	*teaspoon olive oil*
1	*head fennel, finely julienned*
2	*chopped garlic cloves*
1	*large onion, finely chopped*
1	*teaspoon tomato paste*
4	*large tomatoes, peeled, seeded and diced*
1	*bay leaf*
1/2	*bunch thyme, finely chopped*
1/2	*bunch tarragon, finely chopped*

Saute the fennel, garlic and onion in the oil until very soft but with no color. Add the tomato paste and cook for another 2 minutes. Add the diced tomatoes and herbs. Cook slowly for 10 minutes. Season to taste and set aside to cool.

Sauce:

1	*cup fish stock*
6	*chopped shallots*
1	*cup white wine*
2	*cups cream*
1	*pinch saffron*

150

Sweat the shallots in a little butter or oil until soft. Add the wine and reduce down until almost dry. Add the fish stock and bring to a boil again. Add the saffron and reduce the liquid by half. Add the cream and reduce until the sauce coats the back of a spoon. Check seasonings and pass through a fine strainer. Keep hot.

TREES
440 Heliotrope Ave.
Corona del Mar, CA
673-0910

Maryland Style Crab Cakes

1	whole egg
1/2	cup mayonnaise
1/2	teaspoon minced garlic
3-4	splashes of tabasco
2	teaspoons worcestershire sauce
	salt and white pepper to taste
2	pounds backfin lump blue crab meat, cleaned and free of shellbits (comes from Maryland or Louisiana only)
1/2	medium red bell pepper, minced
1/2	medium gold bell pepper, minced
2	stalks celery, minced
1/2	small red onion, minced
1/2	jalapeno peeled and minced
3/4	cup bread crumbs

Combine the egg, mayonnaise, garlic, tabasco and worcestershire, salt and pepper. Mix well to make a sauce. Combine the crabmeat with all of the minced vegetables and add to the sauce. Sprinkle the bread crumbs over the mixture and carefully mix with your hands to combine well. Divide the mixture into 18 parts and each into a biscuit size cake. Preheat oven to 450 degrees. Preheat a skillet with a mixture of half melted butter and oil. Place the crab cakes in the pan and cook to light golden brown on one side. Turn over and place in the oven for 5 minutes. Do not overbrown.

Mustard Cream sauce:

2	teaspoons minced shallots
2	cups dry white wine
2	cups heavy cream
4	tablespoons dijon mustard

In a saucepot, boil the shallots and wine until reduced by 3/4. Stir in the mustard, then the cream. Reduce to desired consistency, strain and serve. Serve the crab cakes with the sauce, creamed corn and fresh green vegetables. Serves six.

TUTTO MARE
545 Fashion Island
Newport Beach, CA
640-6333

Medaglioni di Salmone alla Zarina

1	*7 ounce salmon medallion, 1/4 inch thick*
1	*tablespoon flour*
2	*tablespoons olive oil*
1/2	*ounce leeks, julienne*
2	*tablespoons vodka*
1/2	*ounce caviar, your preference*
1/4	*ounce unsalted butter*
	salt and pepper to taste
1/2	*ounce sun dried tomatoes, julienne*

In a saute pan, warm the olive oil. Cook the salmon for 1 minute on each side. Add the leeks, vodka and caviar. Reduce heat and add the butter to thicken. Serve when the sauce is nice and smooth. Garnish with sun dried tomatoes. Serves one.

Misto Griglia Tutto Mare
(Mixed Seafood Grill)

1 1/2	*pound whole branzino (sea bass), cleaned and scaled*
2	*whole freshwater prawns*
2	*4 ounces of fish filets, your choice*
4	*whole squid tails, cleaned*
1/4	*cup lemon*
2	*tablespoons olive oil*
2	*sprigs basil, chopped*

Over mesquite wood, grill the sea bass until brown. Remove and finish in a oven until done. Time all other seafood to finish at the same time as the sea bass, about 10 minutes. Grill start to finish all the other seafood. Combine lemon juice, olive oil and chopped basil to make a light sauce for the mix grill.

Monkfish with Caramelized Shallot Sauce

1 1/2 pounds monkfish, cleaned and cut into medallions
12   peeled shallots

Place shallots on aluminum foil, season with salt and pepper and drizzle olive oil on the shallots. Wrap tightly, then cover with another piece of foil. Place in a 325 degree oven for 30 minutes. Remove from the oven and reserve all shallots and the liquid. In olive oil, saute the monkfish medallions. Season to taste. Cook about 3 minutes per side. Remove from pan and keep warm. Add shallots and liquid to the pan. Incorporate the sauce. Reserve. To serve, place some leeks on a plate, cover with the medallions and spoon sauce around the medallions. Serve 2 shallots per serving. Garnish with a fresh herb sprig. Serves four.

Sauce:

2   cups white wine
1   sprig thyme
1   sprig rosemary
3   black peppercorns
1   pound butter, softened

In a sauce pot, place the wine, thyme, rosemary and peppercorns. Cook over medium heat until its reduced by 3/4. Cut the butter in pieces and slowly add to the mixture while whisking over medium heat. Strain and reserve in a warm 145 degree bath.

3   leeks, finely sliced

Saute the leeks in butter until soft.

THE CANNERY

3010 Lafayette Ave.
Newport Beach, CA
675-5777

Orange Roughy with Lemon Caper Butter

8	ounce orange roughy filet
2	tablespoons butter
1	tablespoon capers
1	tablespoon lemon juice
1	tablespoon Sauterne wine
1	tablespoon chopped parsley

Coat orange roughy with flour. Melt butter in skillet. Fry roughy on each side to a golden brown. Remove from skillet, keep warm. Add capers, lemon juice and wine to brown butter in skillet. Stir and heat for 2 minutes. Remove from heat and add parsley. Pour over fish. Serves one.

PARADISE CAFE

600 Newport Center Dr.
Newport Beach, CA
644-1237

Paradise Pan Roast

2	small lobster tails, split
3	small clams, cleaned
2	mussels (optional)
1/2	cup clam juice
2	ounces white wine
4	medium scallops
2	large shrimp, peeled and veined
3	ounces of fresh fish, cubed (sea bass, swordfish, or halibut)
3	tablespoons sweet butter
1	tablespoon minced white onion
2	garlic cloves, minced
4	ounces whipping cream
	pinch fresh ground black pepper

In a small sauce pan, cook lobster tails, clams and mussels in the clam juice and white wine until the clams open. Meanwhile, saute scallop, shrimp and fish in the butter for 2 minutes. Drain 3/4 of butter from fish and other shellfish and add onion and garlic. Cook until the garlic just starts turning color (about 2 minutes). Pour in cream and broth from clams and lobster. Heat to almost boiling, add pepper and serve.

McCORMICK & SCHMICK'S

2000 Main St.
Irvine, CA
756-0505

Salmon Broiled with Walnut Basil Salsa

1   7 ounce salmon filet

Charbroil the filet to desired doneness, about 7 to 8 minutes. Top with the sauce and serve. Serves one.

Walnut Basil Salsa:

1   ounce walnut pieces
1   ounce chopped basil
1   ounce chopped cilantro
1   ounce diced tomato
1/2   ounce minced garlic
1/2   ounce chopped red onion
1/2   ounce chopped green pepper
1   ounce olive oil

Combine the above ingredients and mix well.

MONIQUE
31272 Coast Hwy.
Laguna Beach, CA
499-5359

Salmon Grille aux Beurre de Gingenbre
a la Orange
(Grilled Salmon with Ginger-Orange Sauce)

6   8 ounce fresh salmon steaks or filets

Grill salmon on a charcoal broiler for 5 minutes per side. Pour the sauce over the salmon and serve with boiled potatoes and your favorite vegetable. Serves six.

Ginger-Orange Sauce:

1   tablespoon ground fresh ginger
2   cups freshly squeezed orange juice
1   tablespoon fresh cream
2   sprigs oregano
1/2   pound unsalted butter
       salt and white pepper to taste

Combine ginger and orange juice in a pan and reduce. When almost dry, add cream and oregano. Bring to a simmer. Whip in butter over low heat. Season. Do not allow the sauce to boil. This sauce is also good with halibut or any white fish with firm flesh.

THE RITZ

880 Newport Center Dr.
Newport Beach, CA
720-1800

The Ritz is special. It all begins with the red-carpeted valet Welcome to the five distinctive and opulent dining rooms. As elegant as the Ritz is, the classic European cuisine is just as prodigious. Established menu favorites along with daily creations will surely make this dining experience one of lasting memory. The Ritz offers lunch and dinner daily.

Salmon Piccata

12	2 ounces fresh salmon, slices
8	zucchini, 1/4 inch slices
	milk
	seasoned flour
1/2	stick sweet butter
1	cup sliced mushrooms
1	tablespoon capers
	juice of 1/2 of a lemon
1	teaspoon chopped parsley

Dip zucchini and salmon slices, first into milk, then into seasoned flour. Saute in a small amount of hot oil until brown (about 2 minutes on each side.) Arrange alternately on a serving platter. Brown the butter in another skillet, add the mushrooms. Stir and add capers. Add lemon, then spoon over the fish. Garnish with chopped parsley. Serves four.

THE CANNERY

3010 Lafayette Ave.
Newport Beach, CA
675-5777

Seafood Tacos

3	ounces your favorite fish, firm piece
2	corn tortillas, fresh
2	tablespoons salsa, mild or hot
1	tablespoon guacamole
	pinch cilantro
1	tablespoon diced onions
1	Ortega chili, diced (optional)
2	tablespoons grated cheese (jack or cheddar)

Broil fish for 3-4 minutes each side. Heat tortillas (2 per serving) and fill with broiled fish. Top with salsa, onions, chili, guacamole, cilantro and cheese. Hold together with toothpick.

JOHN DOMINIS

2901 W. Coast Hwy.
Newport Beach, CA
650-5112

Seared Black-n-Blue Ahi with Dijon-Soy Sauce

1	7 ounce Hawaiian Ahi, blocked in a 2 inch by 5 inch rectangle
	Cajun Seasoning
2	ounces peanut oil
1	carrot, julienne
1	each red and green bell pepper, julienne
2	slices red onion

Dijon-Soy Sauce:

1	ounce soy sauce
2	teaspoons dijon mustard

Mix together and set aside.

Coat the ahi on all four sides with Cajun seasoning. In a saute pan, bring the peanut oil to a very high heat. Sear ahi on all 4 sides, 20 seconds per side. Remove the ahi from the pan and set aside.

Fill a plastic squirt bottle with the dijon-soy sauce. Cut the ahi in 1/8 inch slices with a very sharp knife. Fan the slices on a dinner plate. With the sauce, paint stripes on the slices length ways. Garnish with the carrots, peppers and red onion. Serve with your choice of pasta. Serves one.

MATTEO'S ITALIAN RESTAURANT

2325 E. Coast Hwy.
Corona del Mar, CA
673-8267

Shrimp Amaretto alla Michelena

10	jumbo shrimp, veined, tails on
2	tablespoons margarine
1	tablespoon minced fresh garlic
1/2	cup chopped onion
1	cup chopped roma tomatoes into 3/4 inch pieces
1	tablespoon chopped fresh basil
2	teaspoons Amaretto liqueur
1	tablespoon clam juice
	salt to taste
	coarsely ground black pepper

Saute shrimp in margarine over medium-low heat, add garlic, cook until shrimp turns pink about 8-10 minutes. Add onion, tomato, basil, Amaretto, clam juice, salt and pepper to taste, and increase to medium heat. Cook 3 minutes and serve on warm plates with steamed zucchini or other fresh steamed vegetables on the side.

BENIHANA
4250 Birch St.
Newport Beach, CA
955-0822

Shrimp with Benihana Ginger Sauce

36	veined large shrimp (16 to 21 count)
1	teaspoon soybean oil
1	tablespoon chopped fresh parsley
1	tablespoon lemon juice

Heat a non-stick skillet. If using an electric skillet, set temperature at 350 degrees. Add oil to the skillet and saute shrimp for 3 minutes per side. Remove the shrimp from the skillet and cut into bite size pieces. Sprinkle with the parsley and return to the skillet. Cook for 1 to 2 minutes more or until opaque in color. Sprinkle with the lemon juice and serve hot with ginger sauce on the side. Serves six.

Ginger sauce:

1/4	cup chopped onion
1	small piece ginger or 1/8 teaspoon ground ginger
1/2	cup soy sauce
1/4	cup rice wine vinegar

Combine all the ingredients in a blender and process until smooth in consistency. Makes 6 servings.

160

DILLMAN'S
801 E. Balboa Blvd.
Balboa, CA
673-7726

Stuffing Mix for Sole or Shrimp

1	onion, chopped
2	bell peppers, chopped
1	pound mushrooms, sliced
1	tablespoon curry powder
2	teaspoons nutmeg
1/4	cup chicken base
1	pound crab meat
1	bunch parsley, finely chopped
1	teaspoon garlic powder
1	teaspoon white pepper
1	teaspoon salt
1	teaspoon worcestershire sauce
1	tablespoon dry mustard
2	cups water
2	cups milk
2	cups butter
2	cups cracker meal
1 1/2	cups bread crumbs

Saute onion, bell pepper and mushroom in butter. Add curry, nutmeg, chicken base, crabmeat and parsley. Simmer for 10 minutes. While simmering, add the rest of the ingredients, except cracker meal and bread crumbs. Add a mixture of flour and water to thicken to desired consistency. Simmer and stir for 5 minutes. Remove from heat and thoroughly mix in cracker meal and bread crumbs. Use to stuff fresh sole filets, shrimp or your favorite fish.

GIORGIO'S LA TRATTORIA

305 Marine Ave.   3012 Newport Blvd.
Balboa Island, CA   Newport Beach, CA
675-6193   673-4020

From Florence in northern Italy, Giorgio brings to Newport a heritage of three generations of expertise in creating Italian dishes. This quiet, unassuming man definitely has a way in a kitchen that will not disappoint you. As with all the better chefs, he creates his own pastas and sauces. He loves to cook at your tableside. If you are looking for down home cooking, Italian style, be sure to stop in at Giorgio's. He is there nightly.

Swordfish alla Giorgio

3/4	pound swordfish steak
2	teaspoons olive oil
	flour, enough to dust the steak
	salt and pepper to taste
1	ounce brandy
2	tomato slices
	basil
	capers
	black olives, sliced

Flour the swordfish steak and saute in olive oil for 30 seconds. Drain oil and combine the rest of the ingredients. Bake in a 400 degree oven for 3 minutes. Serves one.

DILLMAN'S
801 E. Balboa Blvd.
Balboa, CA
673-7726

Turtle Stew

4	pounds turtle meat, cubed into 1 inch pieces
	salt and pepper to taste
3/4	cup flour
1/2	cup oil
1	garlic clove, diced fine
1	large onion, coarsely chopped
6	large potatoes, peeled, cut into 1 1/2 inch pieces
6	carrots, cleaned and cut into 1 1/2 inch pieces
8	stalks celery, diced
24	ounces tomato sauce
3	teaspoons beef base or bouillon
1/2	cup white wine

Season turtle meat with salt and pepper. Thoroughly coat meat with flour. Heat oil in a saute pan and add garlic. Saute garlic until brown and then add the turtle meat. Fast fry until the meat is browned on all sides. Transfer the meat to a large pot or kettle. Add the remaining ingredients and add enough water to just cover the mixture. Simmer covered at low heat for 1 hour, stirring occasionally. Cook until vegetables are tender.

NOTES

ENTREES PASTA

ENTREES PASTA

CARMELO'S RISTORANTE ITALIANO & CONTINENTAL

3520 E. Coast Hwy.
Corona del Mar, CA
675-1922

Agnolotti alla Panna
(Agnolotti with Cream)

Filling:

10	ounces young beet greens or spinach leaves
3	ounces ricotta cheese
3	ounces leftover roast chicken, finely chopped
3	ounces cooked ham, finely chopped
1/4	cup freshly grated parmesan cheese
1	egg
	pinch of freshly grated nutmeg
	salt and freshly ground pepper

Cook beet or spinach leaves in boiling salted water just until wilted. Squeeze dry and chop very finely. In a bowl, combine all filling ingredients. Refrigerate.

Pasta:

2 1/2	cups all purpose flour
3	eggs

Combine flour and eggs and form a dough. Knead until smooth and elastic. Roll out very thinly. Place small balls of filling mixture at 2 1/2 inch intervals over half the sheet of dough. Fold the dough over to cover the filling, pressing the fingers around each ball. Using a pastry wheel with a fluted edge, cut out the agnolotti in half moon or square shapes. Bring a large pot of water to boil over high heat. Drop in the agnolotti and cook al dente.

Sauce:

3	tablespoons butter
1	cup cream
3/4	cup grated fresh Parmesan cheese

While agnolotti is cooking, heat the butter and cream over low heat. Arrange agnolotti on a serving dish and pour butter and cream mixture over the agnolotti. Sprinkle with parmesan cheese and serve.

TUTTO MARE
545 Fashion Island
Newport Beach, CA
640-6333

Bianchi e Neri con Capesante
(Black and White Tagliolini with Scallops)

4	*ounces black and white tagliolini, cooked al dente*
1	*garlic clove, minced*
2	*tablespoons olive oil*
3	*ounces scallops*
1	*teaspoon chopped parsley*
1	*ounce white wine*
2	*ounces seafood based heavy whipping cream*
1	*tablespoon blanched and diced red bell pepper*
1	*teaspoon pink peppercorns*
1	*teaspoon chopped chives*

In a saute pan, saute the garlic in oil, and then add scallops, red pepper and parsley. Toss. Add wine and reduce. Add the seafood based cream; reduce. Continue to toss the mixture. Add the cooked pasta and reduce a bit more. Serve and top with chives and pink peppercorns.

ANTONELLO RISTORANTE
South Coast Plaza Village
1611 W. Sunflower Ave.
Santa Ana, CA
751-7153

Burro Parmiggiano

2/3	*pound spaghetti, cooked al dente*
2	*tablespoons butter at room temperature*
1/4	*cup grated reggiano parmesan cheese*

Toss spaghetti with the butter and parmesan. Serve immediately. Serves two.

RISTORANTE FERRANTELLI

25001 Dana Point Dr.
Dana Point, CA
493-1401

Fettucini Alfredo

1	pound fettucini, cooked al dente, drained
20	ounces heavy whipping cream
1/2	cup butter
1	cup grated parmesan cheese
	salt and cracked pepper to taste

Bring cream to a boil in a skillet and salt and pepper to taste. Add fettucini while the cream is boiling. Slowly add the parmesan until the sauce reaches a desired consistency. Garnish with parsley and parmesan cheese.

RENATO

2304 W. Oceanfront
Newport Beach, CA
673-8058

Fettucini alla Contadina

20	ounces fettucini, cooked al dente
3	tablespoons extra virgin olive oil
7	ounces mild Italian sausage
8	ounces cooked diced chicken breast
2	teaspoons chopped fresh garlic
2	ounces sliced shiitake mushrooms
2	ounces sliced porcini mushrooms
1	teaspoon chopped shallots
1	teaspoon chopped fresh basil
1	tablespoon chicken broth
	pepper to taste

Over a medium flame, saute the sausage and chicken in olive oil until almost done. Add the remaining ingredients. Saute until the vegetables are tender. Toss with fettucini and serve. Serves four.

RUMPELSTILTSKIN'S

114 McFadden Pl.
Newport Beach, CA
673-5025

Lasagna con Pollo
(Mexican Style Chicken Lasagna)

1	whole chicken
1	teaspoon dry oregano
1/2	teaspoon black pepper
1 1/2	cups chopped onion
1	green bell pepper, chopped
2	tablespoons olive oil
3	cups crushed and strained pear tomatoes
1	cup tomato sauce
2	jalapeno pepper, seeded and minced
1	garlic clove, minced
2	tablespoons butter
2	tablespoons flour
1/2	cup milk
1/4	cup whipping cream
1/2	cup chicken broth
2	sheets fresh lasagna, 6 x 16 inches, cooked al dente
1	cup cilantro, chopped
2	pounds ricotta cheese
1	pound cheddar cheese, grated

Season chicken with oregano and black pepper. Roast in an oven at 350 degrees for 2 hours. Remove the meat, discarding bones and skin. Set aside. In a saute pan, saute onions and bell pepper in olive oil until soft. Add tomatoes, tomato sauce, 1 jalapeno and minced garlic. Simmer for 20 minutes.

In another pan, melt butter and whisk in flour until smooth. Cook for 3 minutes, slowly adding milk, whipping cream and chicken broth. Stir until it thickens. Add the tomato mixture, combine and set aside. In a deep lasagna pan, layer as follows: sauce, noodles, chicken, chopped cilantro, jalapeno, sauce, noodles, ricotta cheese, cilantro, jalapeno, noodles, sauce and grated cheddar. Bake 1 hour at 350 degrees. Remove from oven and cool to set. To serve, cut into 8 serving portions. Top with grated cheddar and reheat. Garnish with avocado slices, sour cream and salsa.

VILLA NOVA

3131 W. Coast Hwy.
Newport Beach, CA
642-7880

Linguini alla Daivola

4	ounces fresh linguini, cooked al dente
3	New Zealand Green Lip mussels
8	ounces marinara sauce
	small pinch crushed red chilies
2	tablespoons clam juice
4	ounces scallops
3-4	shrimp

Combine clam juice and chilies. Reduce on flame to 1 tablespoon. Set aside. Blanch mussels in white wine or water. Be sure to remove the beards from the mussels when open. Saute scallops and shrimp in butter. Add marinara and reduced clam juice. Add the mussels and toss with linguini. Serves one.

GIORGIO'S LA TRATTORIA

305 Marine Ave.   3012 Newport Blvd.
Balboa Island, CA   Newport Beach, CA
675-6193   673-4020

Linguini Pescatora

1	tablespoon olive oil
2	garlic cloves, sliced
1	red pepper, seeded and chopped
2	tablespoons fresh parsley, chopped
1/2	cup tomato sauce
3	ounces white wine
	salt and pepper to taste
8	clams, cleaned
8	mussels, cleaned
6	large shrimp, peeled and veined
4	ounces calamari
1/2	pound linguini, cooked al dente

In a large pan, saute garlic in olive oil until brown. Add in next five ingredients. Reduce and simmer 5 minutes. Add in the clams, mussels, shrimp and calamari. Cook until clams open and the shrimp is white. Serve over linguini. Serves two.

ROTHCHILD'S

2407 E. Coast Hwy.
Corona del Mar, CA
673-3750

Linguini Pescatore

1/2	cup olive oil
1	tablespoon chopped garlic
1 1/2	cups sliced mushrooms
2	12 ounce cans baby clams, reserve juice
1 1/2	cups fresh tomato sauce
1	teaspoon chicken base
1/2	cup dry white wine
8	ounces medium sized shrimp, peeled and veined
5	drops tabasco sauce
1/2	pound linguini, cooked al dente
	parmesan cheese

Saute garlic in oil in a large pan. Add mushrooms, juice from clams, tomato sauce and chicken base. Bring to a boil. Add wine, clams and shrimp. Simmer for 6 to 8 minutes. Serve over linguini and top with parmesan cheese.

TUTTO MARE

545 Fashion Island
Newport Beach, CA
640-6333

Mezzelune di Salmone Affumicato
(Smoked Salmon Ravioli with Lemon-Sorrel Sauce)

8   smoked salmon ravioli

Lemon-Sorrel Sauce:

4   ounces seafood base heavy whipping cream
1   teaspoon butter
     juice of 1/2 lemon
2   tablespoons chopped fresh sorrel

In a saute pan, melt butter. Add remaining ingredients and reduce. The finished sauce should be thick, not broken and barely off white in color. Pour over the ravioli.

CIAO MEIN

Hyatt Regency Irvine
17900 Jamboree Rd.
Newport Beach, CA
975-1234

Papardelle

20	*ounces your favorite pasta, cooked al dente*

7	*ounces cooked papardelle*
4	*ounces hot Italian sausage*
5	*wedges roma tomatoes*
1/2	*box roasted red peppers*
1/2	*box roasted yellow pepper*
2	*ounces peas*
1/2	*ounce chopped basil*
1/4	*ounce chopped garlic*
4	*ounces marinara sauce*
1/2	*ounce parmesan*
1/4	*ounce chopped Italian parsley*
1/2	*ounce olive oil*
	salt and pepper to taste

Heat skillet and saute sausage. Add garlic, shallot, sun dried tomatoes and tomato wedges. Add marinara, basil, peas and peppers. Toss pasta with the sauce. Adjust seasoning. Place in a large pasta bowl and garnish with parmesan and parsley. Serves two to four.

RISTORANTE CANTORI

Hyatt Newporter
1107 Jamboree Rd.
Newport Beach, CA
729-1234

Papardelle di Compagnia
(Pasta with Hot Sausage, Peas and Plum Tomatoes)

1	*pound cooked papardelle*
1	*pound hot sausage*
5	*roma tomatoes, diced*
2	*teaspoons chopped garlic*
1	*cup white wine*
10	*basil leaves, chopped*
2	*cups marinara sauce (see below)*
1	*frozen green peas, thawed*

Remove sausage from casings, rough chop, and cook in small amount of oil until cooked through, about 6-8 minutes. Add diced tomatoes, garlic, wine, basil and cook until wine reduces by 2/3. Add marinara sauce and heat through. Add cooked pasta and mix well. Just before serving add peas.

Marinara sauce:

3	*ounces olive oil*
1	*small onion, diced*
1/2	*cup chopped fresh basil*
1	*tablespoon chopped fresh oregano*
2	*pounds fresh roma tomatoes, rough chopped*
2	*12 ounce cans whole plum tomatoes*
1/2	*tablespoon chopped garlic*
1/4	*cup sugar*
	salt and white pepper to taste

Saute onions in oil until transparent. Add garlic, basil, oregano, fresh tomatoes and canned tomatoes. Cook 25-30 minutes over low heat. Season with sugar, salt and white pepper. Place in a blender and puree, keeping a chunky consistency. Keep warm for pasta. Yields 2 quarts.

MATTEO'S
2325 E. Coast Hwy.
Corona del Mar, CA
673-8267

Pasta with Avelino Pesto

1/4   *cup extra virgin olive oil*
4   *ounces pine nuts*
1   *tablespoon minced fresh garlic*
4   *tablespoons chopped fresh basil*
1   *pound linguini or vermicelli, cooked al dente*
1/4   *cup grated romano cheese*
1/4   *teaspoon red pepper, optional*

Heat oil in a large skillet or saute pan over medium-low heat. Add pine nuts and garlic, saute until nuts begin to brown slightly. Add basil and remove from the heat. Toss with cooked pasta. Add cheese and red pepper. Toss, then serve.

ANTONELLO RISTORANTE
South Coast Plaza Village
1611 W. Sunflower Ave.
Santa Ana, CA
751-7153

Penne alla Vodka

2/3   *pound penne, cooked al dente*
8   *ounces cream*
6   *ounces pureed tomatoes*
1   *tablespoon chopped shallots*
4   *ounces vodka*
1/2   *cup grated parmesan cheese*
2   *tablespoons extra virgin olive oil*

Heat olive oil and saute shallots for 30 seconds. Deglaze with vodka, flame and reduce by half. Add cream and reduce by half over medium heat. Add tomatoes and parmesan. Cook for 2 minutes. Salt and pepper to taste. Add the penne and cook an additional minute. Serve immediately. Serves two.

THE TALE OF THE WHALE
Balboa Pavilion
400 Main St.
Balboa, CA
673-4633

Seafood Fettucini

3	garlic cloves, minced
1	green bell pepper, seeded, and chopped
1	onion, chopped
1	16 ounce can of crushed tomatoes
1/2	cup white wine
1/4	tablespoon sweet basil
1/4	tablespoon oregano
1/4	tablespoon thyme
	pinch fennel seed
	salt and pepper to taste
1	8 ounce can chopped clams
1/4	pound shrimp, peeled, veined
1/4	pound scallops
1/4	pound crabmeat
1/4	pound swordfish, cut to bite size pieces
4	pounds fettucini, cooked al dente

In a saucepan, saute the garlic, bell pepper and onion until the onion is transparent. Add wine, tomatoes and spices. Simmer over low heat for 1 hour. Add the seafood. Cook until shrimp turns white. Serve over fettucini. Serves 4.

MAXI'S GRILLE

Red Lion Inn, Orange County Airport
3050 Bristol St.
Costa Mesa, CA
540-7000

Smoked Chicken with Angel Hair

24	ounces smoked chicken breast, sliced thin
1/2	cup finely diced onion
1	teaspoon mashed garlic
4	ounces olive oil
24	black Nicoise olives
8	ounces Greek feta cheese
2	tablespoons fresh chopped herbs
8	teaspoons sun dried tomatoes, julienne
48	ounces angel hair pasta, cooked al dente

Saute the onions and garlic in the olive oil. When the onions are translucent, add the smoked chicken. Saute until the chicken is warmed and then add the remaining ingredients except for the pasta. Heat for 1 to 2 minutes then twist in the pasta. Remove the pasta and place on an oval platter. Lay the rest of the ingredients on top. Garnish with fresh herbs and grated parmesan cheese. Serves four.

THE QUIET WOMAN

3224 E. Coast Hwy.
Corona del Mar, CA
640-7440

Swordfish Pasta

2	tablespoons sweet butter
4	large shallots, diced small
	juice of 1/2 lemon
1/4	cup dry vermouth
1	pint heavy cream
1/4	cup sundried tomatoes, diced
1/2	bunch fresh tarragon, finely chopped
1 1/2	pounds swordfish steak
3	pounds linguini, cooked al dente
1/8	cup finely chopped parsley

Melt butter in a large saute pan. Add diced shallots and saute over low heat for 10 minutes. Add juice of lemon, dry vermouth and heavy cream. Bring to a boil and reduce by 1/3. When sauce begins to thicken, add diced tomatoes and tarragon. Simmer until mixture thickens. Charbroil swordfish and cut into 1 1/2 inch chunks. Place chunks on a bed of linguini. Pour sauce over swordfish. Garnish with chopped parsley. Serves four.

ROTHCHILD'S

2407 E. Coast Hwy.
Corona del Mar, CA
673-3750

Rigatoni con Broccoli

1/2	cup olive oil
1	tablespoon garlic, chopped
1/4	pound prosciutto ham, julienne
1 1/2	cups sliced mushrooms
1 1/2	cups tomato sauce
2	cups water
1	teaspoon chicken base
1 1/2	bunches broccoli, chopped
5	drops tabasco
1/4	cup parmesan cheese
	rigatoni, cooked al dente

Saute garlic and ham in olive oil. Add mushrooms, tomato sauce, water, tabasco and chicken base. Bring to a boil. Add broccoli and simmer for 6-8 minutes. Serve over cooked pasta. Top with the parmesan cheese.

STUFT NOODLE

215 Riverside Ave.
Newport Beach, CA
646-2333

Tortellini Angelo

2	*ounces olive oil*
1 1/2	*teaspoons diced shallots*
1	*teaspoon chopped garlic*
3	*ounces prosciutto, diced*
12	*ounces chicken, cut to bite size pieces*
2	*scallions, diced*
1/2	*pound mushrooms, sliced*
1	*ounce white wine*
16	*ounces heavy cream*
1/4	*teaspoon black pepper*
1	*tablespoon butter*
2	*tablespoons parmesan*
2	*tablespoons chopped fresh basil*
1	*pound tortellini, cooked al dente*

Heat olive oil in a saute pan. Add shallots, garlic, prosciutto and saute for 1 minute. Add chicken, scallions, mushrooms; saute 1 minute. Add wine to deglaze the pan. Add cream, pepper, butter, parmesan and basil. Simmer sauce on medium heat for 5 minutes. Add tortellini. Stir well and serve. Serves four.

DESSERTS

DESSERTS

EL TORITO GRILL

951 Newport Center Dr.
Newport Beach, CA
640-2875

Banana Empanadas with Ice Cream and Caramel Sauce

Filling:

1 1/2	ounces unsalted butter
2	ounces nuts, finely chopped
1	tablespoon ground cinnamon
4	tablespoons granulated sugar
4	large ripe bananas, sliced
4	flour tortillas, 9 inch diameter

Melt butter in heavy saucepan, combine the nuts, cinnamon, sugar and bananas and saute together for 5 minutes. Cool, then divide into four portions. Put one portion in the center of each tortilla, roll, tucking in ends as for a burrito. Secure seam edge with a toothpick. May be covered with plastic and refrigerated for hours at this point.

Caramel sauce:

1	cup granulated sugar
1/2	cup water
1/2	teaspoon lime juice
1 1/2	ounces unsalted butter
8	ounces heavy cream

Mix sugar, water and lime juice together in a heavy sauce pan. Cook together over low heat until the sugar is caramelized. Add cream and butter slowly, whisking together until thick. May also be refrigerated, and heated gently when ready for use.

To serve: Heat delicate oil, such as corn or sunflower, in a vessel for deep-frying. Fry each empanada until golden brown and crisp. Cool slightly, then cut each into three portions and serve, two for each plate, topped with caramel sauce and a scoop of ice cream. Serves 6.

THE ARCHES

3334 W. Coast Hwy.
Newport Beach, CA
645-7077

Bananas Foster

2 1/2   cups brown sugar
1/4   teaspoon ground cinnamon
1/4   cup butter
1/2   teaspoon rum
1/4   cup banana liqueur
2   bananas, sliced
2   tablespoons brandy
2   scoops vanilla ice cream

Place brown sugar and cinnamon in crepe pan or skillet, when hot add butter. When butter is melted, add rum. Stir, add banana liqueur. Stir and let mixture caramelize. Add sliced bananas, cover with the sauce. Place a scoop of ice cream into separate bowls. Top ice cream with the bananas only. Add brandy to the sauce in the pan. Over a very high flame, ignite brandy and spoon flaming sauce over the ice cream and bananas.

RISTORANTE FERRANTELLI

25001 Dana Point Dr.
Dana Point, CA
493-1401

Cannoli Siciliani

10   prepared cannoli shells, available at Italian delicatessens
1/2   pound ricotta cheese
1/2   cup dried fruit
4   tablespoons Anisette
4   tablespoons powdered sugar

Combine the ricotta, fruit, Anisette and powdered sugar. Mix with a fork or pastry blender until it reaches a creamy consistency. Stuff the shells and dust with powdered sugar. Serves ten.

THE CHART HOUSE

2801 W. Coast Hwy.   34442 Green Lantern
Newport Beach, CA   Dana Point, CA
548-5889   493-1183

Chart House Mud Pie

1/2	package Nabisco Chocolate Wafers
1/2	cube butter, melted
1	gallon coffee ice cream
1 1/2	cups fudge sauce
	whipped cream
	slivered almonds

Crush wafers and add butter. Mix well. Press into 9 inch pie plate. Cover with soft coffee ice cream. Put into freezer until ice cream is firm. Top with cold fudge sauce (it helps to place fudge sauce in freezer for a time to make spreading easier.) Store mud pie in freezer about 10 hours. To serve, slice the pie into 8 portions and serve on a chilled dessert plate with a chilled fork. Top with whipped cream and slivered almonds.

WATERCOLORS

Dana Point Resort
25135 Park Lantern
Dana Point, CA
661-5000

Chocolate Decadence

2	ounces butter
1	teaspoon vanilla
1	cup sugar
2	eggs, separated
2	ounces melted chocolate
2	tablespoons hot water
1/3	cup flour
1/8	teaspoon salt

Cream the butter and add the vanilla and sugar. Beat in the egg yolks and chocolate until smooth. Add water first, then the flour and beat until smooth. Beat the egg whites until stiff and mix with the chocolate. Put in a mold and bake at 325 degrees for 20 minutes. Cool and glaze with chocolate icing and shavings. Serve on pureed raspberries and mint leaf.

RUMPELSTILTSKIN'S
114 McFadden Pl.
Newport Beach, CA
673-5025

Chocolate Mousse Pie

Filling:

1/3	cup sugar
1/3	cup water
1 1/2	cup semi-sweet chocolate bits
3	egg whites
1/3	cup Amaretto
4	cups whipping cream

Cook sugar with water in saucepan until syrup turns a pale golden. Melt chocolate with Amaretto over double boiler. Beat egg whites until stiff, then slowly add syrup, beating constantly. Slowly add melted chocolate. Cool mixture for 2 hours in refrigerator. Whip cream until stiff and fold into chocolate mixture.

Crust:

2	cups Oreo cookies, crumbled
1/2	cup butter, melted
1/4	cup sugar
1/2	cup almonds, chopped or sliced

Mix the cookie crumbs, melted butter and sugar to make a crust. Press into a spring pan. Add filling and top with almonds. Freeze pie for 24 hours. To serve, top with whipped cream and shaved chocolate

TREES
440 Heliotrope Ave.
Corona del Mar, CA
673-0910

Cream Cheese Cake

Crust:

2 1/2	cups graham cracker crumbs
3/4	cup ground almonds
6	ounces melted butter
2	tablespoons honey

Preheat oven to 350 degrees. In a food processor, combine crumbs, almonds, butter and honey. Mix together with the metal chopping blade until well combined. Press the mixture into a 10" spring pan. Use your fingers to distribute the mixture evenly throughout the pan, covering the bottom and sides equally. Be sure to press the mixture firmly in place as this will be the structure of the cake. Refrigerate for 1 hour.

Filling:

4	eggs
24	ounces cream cheese
1/3	cup sugar
1	teaspoon pure vanilla extract
	peel of 1 lemon, grated fine

Using a food processor with a metal chopping blade, combine the eggs, cream cheese, sugar, vanilla and lemon rind. When smooth and creamy, pour the mixture into the crust and bake for 25 to 30 minutes or until the filling has set.

Topping:

1	pint sour cream
1/2	cup sugar
1	teaspoon pure vanilla extract
1	egg white

Whip in a stainless steel bowl, the sour cream with sugar, vanilla and egg white to make the topping. Remove the cake from the oven and carefully "float" the mixture on top of the filling, being careful not to break through the filling. Immediately place the cake back into the oven for 8-10 minutes. Remove from the oven and cool in the refrigerator for at least 3 to 4 hours before removing the pan and serving.

THE RITZ
880 Newport Center Dr.
Newport Beach, CA
720-1800

Creme Brulee

10	ramekins filled 1/3 full with fruit of the season
1	quart heavy cream
8	ounces granulated sugar
24	egg yolks

Heat cream in a large saucepot to boiling point. Turn off heat and keep hot. In a large bowl, mix with a strong whip, the egg yolks and sugar until well combined. Slowly pour hot cream into egg mixture, constantly whipping by hand (this warms the eggs and helps prevent curdling). Pour everything back into saucepot and cook over medium heat, whipping continuously. When quite thick around sides of saucepot and ready to boil, quickly pour the custard into a waiting bowl, stir often. Ladle into ramekins immediately, and chill until set (about 30 minutes). Sprinkle with sugar and caramelize under a broiler. Serve or refrigerate up to 1 hour. Serves 10.

TETE A TETE
217 Marine Ave.
Balboa Island, CA
673-0570

Creme Brulee with Raspberries

7	*egg yolks*
1/4	*cup light brown sugar*
1/4	*granulated sugar*
3	*cups heavy whipping cream*
1	*vanilla bean*
	pinch of salt
	fresh raspberries
	mint leaf
	powdered sugar

Mix egg yolks and sugars together. Bring the cream, vanilla and salt to a boil and stir into the egg mixture. Mix well until the sugar dissolves. Pour the mixture into 6 oven safe ramekins and top each with water so that the ramekins are 3/4 full. Poach in a oven at 350 degrees for 40 minutes. Remove and let cool down or refrigerate. Before serving, sprinkle with granulated sugar and flame the top with either a torch or under the broiler. Garnish with raspberries, mint leaf and powdered sugar. Serves six.

FIVE CROWNS

3801 E. Coast Hwy.
Corona del Mar, CA
760-0331

English Trifle *

1	package (4 1/2 ounces) vanilla pudding mix
2	cups half and half
2	tablespoons dark rum
2	cup whipping cream
3	tablespoons sugar
4	tablespoons red raspberry preserves
1	10 inch round sponge cake
1/4	cup dry sherry
1/4	cup brandy
1 1/2	cups sliced strawberries
15	whole strawberries

Combine pudding mix and half and half. Cook, stirring constantly until mixture comes to a boil and thickens. Add rum and chill. Whip 1 cup whipping cream until stiff and fold into chilled pudding. Coat the inside of a deep 10 inch glass bowl with raspberry preserves to within 1 inch of top. Slice cake horizontally into fourths. Place top slice, crust side up, in bottom of bowl, curving edges of cake upwards. Combine brandy and sherry, sprinkle 2 tablespoons over cake. Spread 1/3 of chilled pudding mixture over cake. Scatter over 1/2 cup sliced strawberries. Repeat procedure two additional times. Cover with remaining cake layer, crust side down and sprinkle with remaining brandy/sherry mixture. Whip remaining 1 cup whipping cream with 2 tablespoons sugar until stiff. Place in pastry bag with fluted tip. Cover top with rosettes of cream and decorate with whole strawberries. Chill at least 6 hours. Serves 12.

* Variation of restaurant recipe

THE WINE CELLAR

Hyatt Newporter
1107 Jamboree Rd.
Newport Beach, CA
729-1234

Feuillete aux Fruits Rouges a la Creme Mousseline
(Fresh Fruits in Puff Pastry with Custard Sauce)

4	4 x 4 inch pieces puff pastry (available at specialty store)
8	ounces pastry cream (see below)
1	basket raspberries
1	basket blueberries
1	basket strawberries, sliced
1	papaya, sliced

Prick pastry with a fork, slightly. Mix one egg yolk with 2 tablespoons water. Brush mixture on pastry. Bake in 375 degree oven until golden brown for 5-7 minutes. Remove and set aside to cool. Spread about 2 ounces of pastry cream on cooked pastry. Arrange fruits on top of cream.

Pastry cream:

8	ounces milk
3	ounces sugar
2	drops vanilla extract
3	egg yolks
1	ounce corn starch
2	teaspoons gelatine powder
1	teaspoon cold water
2	ounces unsalted butter, room temperature

In a small pan, add milk, half the sugar, and vanilla. Bring to a boil. Remove from heat. Mix water and gelatine together and set aside. In a small bowl, put egg yolks, corn starch and remaining sugar and mix well. Slowly pour milk into egg yolk mixture, stirring constantly. Add back to pan and cook over medium heat for 2-3 minutes. Mixture should start to thicken. Be careful not to overheat the sauce. Remove from heat and add softened gelatine. Stir in softened butter, piece by piece, stirring constantly, until all butter is melted. Pour into clean bowl. Refrigerate until completely cold.

JAMBOREE CAFE

Hyatt Newporter
1107 Jamboree Rd.
Newport Beach, CA
729-1234

Fresh Berries with Creme Fraiche

2	each 1/2" slice pound cake
8	ounces mixed fresh berries, quartered strawberries, raspberries, blackberries and blueberries
1	ounce Grand Marnier
4	ounces Creme Fraiche

Place slices of pound cake on plate. Mix berries together and place half on cake and half on the plate. Sprinkle Grand Marnier on the cake. Spoon Creme Fraiche over cake and berries. Garnish with fresh mint. Serves two.

MONIQUE

31727 Coast Hwy.
Laguna Beach, CA
499-5359

Fresh Fruit Terrine with Raspberry Sauce

1 1/3	cups unsalted butter
1 1/3	cups sugar
1 3/4	cups almond powder
4	eggs
1	pear or apple, peeled and diced
1	kiwi, peeled and diced
2/3	cup raspberries or blackberries
1	tablespoon pistachios
1	pint strawberries

Whip butter in a mixer until soft. Slowly add sugar while still whipping. Add the almond powder and eggs. Fold in all the fruit with a plastic spatula and pack into bread pans. Cover tightly with plastic wrap and refrigerate for 24 hours. Unmold by setting pan in a water bath and turn upside down on a plate. Slice like a loaf of bread. Spoon on raspberry sauce.

Raspberry sauce:

2 1/2   *pints fresh raspberries*
1/3   *cup sugar*
1   *tablespoon Chambord liqueur*

Combine all the ingredients and cook slowly until the raspberries fall apart. Put the sauce in a food processor and puree until smooth. (Blackberries, strawberries or blueberries may be substituted).

CLAES'

Hotel Laguna
425 S. Coast Hwy.
Laguna Beach, CA
494-1151

Grapefruit-Tarragon Sorbet

        juice of 4 grapefruits
3/4   *cup sugar*
1/4   *cup water*
3   *tablespoons fresh chopped tarragon*

Mix grapefruit juice with the sugar and water. Freeze in a ice cream machine. After processed, fold in chopped tarragon. Serve with grapefruit sections.

Mango Sorbet

2   *fresh mangos, peeled and seeded*
1/2   *cup sugar*
1/4   *cup water*
        juice of 2 lemons
6   *Borage flowers*

Mix all the ingredients in a blender. Freeze in an ice cream machine. Upon serving, garnish with sliced mango and Borage flowers.

FIVE CROWNS
3801 E. Coast Hwy.
Corona del Mar, CA
760-0331

Mango Sorbet with Tequila and Lime

1	cup water
3/4	cup sugar
	juice of 1 lime
3-4	ripe mangos (approximately 1 3/4 pounds)
1 1/2	ounces tequila

Place water, sugar and lime juice in a small saucepan and bring to a boil to dissolve sugar. Remove from heat to cool completely. Peel skin from mangos and remove the flesh from the seeds. In a blender, process mango pulp and tequila to a puree. Combine with sugar syrup. Freeze in ice cream or sorbet machine according to manufacturer's directions. Serves 6-8.

THE OLD DANA POINT CAFE
24720 Del Prado Ave.
Dana Point, CA
661-6003

Pam's Peanut Butter Pie

Crust:

1 1/3	cups graham cracker crumbs
1/3	cup brown sugar
1/2	teaspoon cinnamon
1/3	cup melted butter

Combine the above ingredients until crumbly. With the back of a spoon, press to the bottom and sides of a well greased 9 inch pie pan. Chill well.

194

Filling:

6   *ounces softened cream cheese*
3/4   *cup powdered sugar*
1/2   *cup chunky peanut butter*
1   *8 ounce container "Cool Whip"*

Cream together the cream cheese, peanut butter and powdered sugar. Fold in the "Cool Whip". Do not stir too much as it will melt down. Fill the pie shell and put in the freezer to set. Set out 15 to 20 minutes before serving. Serves six.

PAVILION

Four Seasons Hotel
690 Newport Center Dr.
Newport Beach, CA
759-0808

"Pavilion" Zucchini Walnut Bread

4 1/4   *cups vegetable oil*
3   *cups sugar*
1 1/2   *cups eggs*
4 3/4   *cups flour*
2   *tablespoons and 2 teaspoons baking powder*
2   *teaspoons cinnamon*
1   *teaspoon vanilla extract*
2   *teaspoons salt*
4   *large zucchini, seeded and grated*
1   *cup chopped walnuts*
1/2   *cup half and half*

In a mixing bowl, combine oil, sugar, eggs and vanilla extract. Sift flour, salt, baking powder and cinnamon and add to the egg mixture. Mix well. Add the grated zucchini. Be sure to squeeze out excess moisture before adding. Add the chopped walnuts. Gradually add the half and half. Pour into a greased bread pan. Bake at 325 degrees for 45 minutes to 1 hour or until a toothpick comes out clean.

BLUE BEET CAFE
107 21st. Pl.
Newport Beach, CA
675-2338

Raspberry Delight

12	*ounces fresh raspberries*
4	*tablespoons sugar*
3	*ounces raspberry liqueur*
3	*ounces sweet red wine*
1/2	*teaspoon gelatin powder*
1	*cup whipped cream*

Crush berries in a blender. Add sugar, wine and liqueur. Strain to remove seeds. To prepare the gelatin, dissolve gelatin in 1/4 cup of water and heat slightly. Combine mixture with the berries. Fold into the whipped cream. Fill dessert glasses. Top with fresh raspberries, whipped cream and grated chocolate. Serves six.

PAVILION
Four Seasons Hotel
690 Newport Center Dr.
Newport Beach, CA
759-0808

Raspberry and Lemon Cream Napoleon

3	*pints fresh raspberries*
2	*cups lemon cream*
18	*Napoleon wafers*

Lemon cream:

2 1/2	*egg yolks*
3	*eggs*
1 3/4	*cups sugar*
1	*lemon, zested*
1/2	*cup lemon juice*
8	*tablespoons butter*

In a stainless steel bowl, combine the eggs, sugar, lemon zest and juice. Cook over a double boiler at a medium heat until it thickens. Remove from the stove, whisk in butter. Strain and cool completely.

Napoleon wafers:

6	tablespoons butter, softened
3/4	cup powdered sugar
3	egg whites
1/2	cup cake flour

Beat butter with the powdered sugar until fluffy. Add egg whites, one at a time. Mix well after each egg white is added. Add flour and mix well. Preheat oven to 350 degrees. Spread batter into 3 inch circles on a greased cookie sheet. You will need to make 18. Bake until lightly browned. Remove from cookie sheet and cool on a flat surface.

To assemble: On 6 of the wafers, spread a 1/4 inch layer of the lemon cream. Arrange whole raspberries to cover the lemon cream. Place another wafer on top of the berries. Again, spread lemon cream on the top wafer and add more raspberries. Place the last 6 wafers on each of the stacks. Dust with powdered sugar. Serve with raspberry sauce.

THE PALM GARDEN

Sheraton Hotel, Newport Beach
4545 MacArthur Blvd.
Newport Beach, CA
833-0570

Raspberry, Strawberry and Blueberry Sabayon Parfait

2	baskets raspberries
2	baskets strawberries
2	baskets blueberries
12	egg yolks
3	cups sugar
3	cups marsala
1	quart whipping cream
1	tablespoon vanilla
1/2	cup powdered sugar

Whisk egg yolks, sugar and marsala over a double boiler until a thick custard forms. Remove from heat and refrigerate. In a separate bowl, beat whipping cream, vanilla and powdered sugar until stiff peaks form. When the custard is cool, fold in whipped cream mixture. In tall glasses, alternate layers of berries with the sauce sabayon.

THE QUIET WOMAN

3224 E. Coast Hwy.
Corona del Mar, CA
640-7440

Toll House Pie

1	stick of butter
1	teaspoon pure vanilla
2	beaten eggs
1	cup sugar
1/2	cup flour
1	cup walnuts
1	cup chocolate chips
1	deep dish pie shell

Melt the butter over low heat and add vanilla. Set aside. Mix the eggs and sugar until smooth, do not whip. Add the flour and mix until smooth. Put the egg and flour mixture into a large saucepan and add the butter and vanilla mixture. Continuously stir while reheating. When the mixture is thoroughly mixed and warm, add the walnuts and chocolate chips. Immediately pour the mixture into a pie shell. Bake at 325 degrees for 1 hour.

GULLIVER'S
18482 MacArthur Blvd.
Irvine, CA
833-8411

Trifle

4	ounces raspberry preserves
	sponge cake, cut into 4 slices
1	quart puree pastry cream
2	tablespoons Appleton dark rum
1 1/2	pints whipping cream
6	cups fresh or defrosted raspberries
	fresh strawberries for garnish, washed and halved

Coat the inside of a large bowl with preserves. Blend the rum, whipped cream and pastry cream. Place a slice of cake at the bottom of the bowl and sprinkle lightly with rum. Coat each layer with the preserves. Spread 12 ounces of pastry cream and sprinkle 2 cups raspberries evenly. Repeat twice more for each layer. Finish the top layer with the 4th slice. Fill a pastry bag with whipped cream and decorate. Garnish with fresh strawberries. Yields twelve portions.

ANTOINE
Le Meridien Hotel, Newport Beach
4500 MacArthur Blvd.
Newport Beach, CA
476-2001

Warm Flourless Chocolate Cake

14	ounces bitter chocolate (Valrona Caraibe)
14	ounces butter
6	beaten egg yolks
1	whole egg
14	ounces sugar
13	egg whites

In a bowl or saucepan, melt chocolate in a double boiler. Add butter and mix well. Remove from heat. In another bowl, combine the whole egg with the yolks and 1/2 of the sugar. Slowly blend with the chocolate mixture. Keep warm. Whisk the egg whites and add the remaining sugar. Whisk until firm, like a meringue. Fold in the chocolate mixture, slowly and carefully to ensure fluffiness of the mixture. Pour into a greased baking dish (15" x 20" x 1" high). Bake at 300 degrees for 30 minutes or until done. While still warm, cut to desired servings. Reheat prior to serving. Dust with powdered sugar and serve with creme anglaise or ice cream. Serves eight.

NOTE: This cake has to be made and served the same day. It cannot be kept for a long period of time.

VILLA NOVA
3131 W. Coast Hwy.
Newport Beach, CA
642-7880

Zabaione

3   egg yolks
1 1/2 tablespoons sugar
1   tablespoon warm water
2   tablespoons marsala wine (Florio Golden Marsala)

In a metal mixing bowl, combine the above ingredients. Hold the bowl over a slow boiling pot of water until thick. Makes 1 to 2 three ounce servings.

POTPOURRI

POTPOURRI

FAR PAVILLIONS

1520 W. Coast Hwy.
Newport Beach, CA
548-7167

Far Pavillions features Northern India cuisine. Specialties include Shrimp Far Pavillions and Bihari Kabab. The atmosphere is a quiet and casual ambiance. This truly unique restaurant offers an exceptional menu to fascinate anyone that is looking for something other than the standard fare most restaurants offer. Far Pavillions is open for lunch during the week, and dinner nightly.

Bharta
(Eggplant Souffle)

1	large eggplant
2	large onions, chopped
2-3	medium tomatoes, diced
1/2	cup peas
4	tablespoons vegetable oil
3/4	teaspoon paprika
1/2	teaspoon cayenne pepper
1/2	teaspoon turmeric
1/2	teaspoon curry powder
	salt to taste
1/2	cup dry cilantro

Coat the eggplant with oil and roast at 375 degrees in an oven for 15-20 minutes or until skin is completely wrinkled and has changed color. Peel skin off the eggplant under cold running water. Mash eggplant fine and set aside.

In a heavy saucepan, heat 4 tablespoons of oil and add onions and tomato. Cook for 3-4 minutes on medium-high flame. Add peas and all the seasonings except for the dry cilantro and cook for another 3-4 minutes. Add mashed eggplant and 1/2 cup of water. Cook on a low flame for 10-12 minutes or until eggplant is completely soft. Put on a serving dish and garnish with dry cilantro.

THE QUIET WOMAN

3224 E. Coast Hwy.
Corona del Mar, CA
640-7440

Butternut Squash

1   butternut squash, peeled, seeded and cut into about 8 pieces
1/4   cup butter
1/4   cup brown sugar
      salt and pepper to taste

Steam (do not boil) squash until a fork easily penetrates the squash. Add the butter, brown sugar and season to taste. With an electric mixer, blend until smooth.

THE RITZ

880 Newport Center Dr.
Newport Beach, CA
720-1800

Creamed Corn

2   10 ounce packages frozen kernel corn
1   cup whipping cream
1   cup milk
1   teaspoon salt
1/4   teaspoon M.S.G. (Accent), optional
6   teaspoons sugar
      pinch white or cayenne pepper
2   tablespoons melted butter
2   tablespoons flour

Combine all ingredients except for the butter and flour. Bring mixture to a boil and simmer 5 minutes. Blend the butter with the flour and add to the corn and mix well. Remove from heat. Variation: Put finished corn in heat proof casserole, sprinkle with Parmesan cheese. Place under a broiler until evenly browned. Serves eight.

FIVE CROWNS
3801 E. Coast Hwy.
Corona del Mar, CA
760-0331

*Creamed Spinach**

2	10 ounce packages frozen chopped spinach, thawed
4	finely chopped slices bacon
1/2	cup finely chopped Spanish onion
1/2	cup finely chopped green onion
2	minced garlic cloves
4	tablespoons flour
1	cup milk
1	cup half and half
1 1/2	teaspoon salt
1/2	teaspoon pepper

Squeeze water from thawed spinach and set aside. Slowly fry bacon and onions together until onions are tender (about 10 minutes). Add garlic. Remove from heat, add flour and blend thoroughly. Slowly add the milk and cream stirring constantly, add seasonings. Return to heat and stir until thickened. Add spinach, mix thoroughly and simmer 5 minutes. Serves six.

* Variation of restaurant recipe.

HASSAN'S CAFE
3325 Newport Blvd.
Newport Beach, CA
675-4668

Kousa Meshie
(Stuffed Zucchini)

8	zucchini, medium size
1/2	pound ground lamb or beef
1/4	cup short grain rice
1/2	cup chopped onions
2	garlic cloves, chopped
1	tomato, chopped
1	16 ounce can of tomato sauce
	lamb bones or ribs
	dash of cinnamon, salt and pepper

Mix rice, onions, ground meat, garlic and tomato with salt, pepper and cinnamon. Cut off the head of zucchini, with the back of the spoon, take out all the of the meat to make room for stuffing. Stuff the zucchini with the meat and rice mixture to only 3/4 full in order to leave room for the rice to cook and expand. Put the bones on the bottom of the pot and lay the zucchini over them, cover with tomato sauce and season with salt, pepper and the cinnamon. Cook for 25 minutes over medium heat and serve hot.

ANTONELLO RISTORANTE
South Coast Plaza Village
1611 W. Sunflower Ave.
Santa Ana, CA
751-7153

Patate Rostite

8	new red potatoes, quartered
4	whole garlic cloves
2	sprigs rosemary
1/2	cup olive oil
	salt and pepper to taste

Heat olive oil in a skillet. When the oil is hot, add all the ingredients and saute for 2 minutes. Place in a 400 degree oven and bake for 15 to 20 minutes until golden brown.

WATERCOLORS

Dana Point Resort
25135 Park Lantern
Dana Point, CA
661-5000

Potato Frittata

4	*ounces potatoes, peeled and shredded*
1 1/2	*tablespoons eggplant, julienne*
1 1/2	*tablespoons zucchini, julienne*
	grated romano cheese
1/2	*beaten egg*
1	*ounce heavy cream*
	salt and pepper to taste

Combine all the ingredients and put into a mold. Bake 15 minutes at 375 degrees. Serves one.

THE WINE CELLAR

Hyatt Newporter
1107 Jamboree Rd.
Newport Beach, CA
729-1234

Ratatouille aux Coriander Frais
(Ratatouille with Fresh Cilantro Sauce)

1	*small eggplant, diced*
1	*small white onion, diced*
1	*each green and yellow zucchini, diced*
1	*each red and green bell peppers, diced*
2	*roma tomatoes, diced*
3	*ounces olive oil*
4	*leaves fresh basil*
1	*teaspoon chopped fresh garlic*
	salt and pepper to taste

Heat oil in a pan, add onions and saute 1 minute. Add zucchini, peppers and eggplant. Saute until vegetables start to soften. Add tomatoes, garlic, basil and season with salt and pepper. Remove from heat and hold. Keep warm until ready to serve.

Fresh Coriander sauce:

1	pound unsalted butter
1	ounce shallots, chopped
	juice of 1 lemon
2	cups white wine
1/2	cup heavy cream
	salt and white pepper to taste
1	bunch fresh coriander (cilantro)

Cube butter in small pieces. Set aside. In a saute pan, saute shallots in small amount of butter for 1 minute. Add white wine and lemon juice. Reduce to syrup consistency. Add heavy cream and reduce by 1/2. Reduce heat to low temperature and slowly add butter to sauce, piece by piece, stirring constantly with a whip until all butter is added. Remove from heat and keep stirring until all pieces of butter have melted. Season with salt and white pepper. Strain sauce through fine sieve into a container. Chop the cilantro leaves and add to the strained sauce. Keep in a warm spot until ready to use. Note: Recommended to be served with the braised swordfish with zucchini scales (see seafood entrees).

LE BIARRITZ
414 N. Old Newport Blvd.
Newport Beach, CA
645-6700

Le Biarritz is a restaurant that lies just off the beaten path. Le Biarritz is located up the hill from the intersection of Coast Highway and Newport Blvd. The awards and recognition that this restaurant has earned, speaks well of its proprietor, Yuan Humbert, and his accomplishments. If you are tired of dealing with the hubbub of Newport, need quiet, go up the hill and enjoy the service and excellent French-Swiss cuisine.

Ratatouille Nicoise

1	green bell pepper, seeded, cut into 1/2 inch squares
3	yellow onions, sliced thinly
3	garlic cloves, peeled and crushed
2	tablespoons olive oil
3	medium zucchini, sliced 1/4 inch thick
1	medium eggplant, cut 1/4 inch thick, and 1/2 inch wide
3	tomatoes, blanched, peeled, seeded and quartered
2	laurel leaves
1	teaspoon thyme

In a saute pan, saute bell pepper, onions and garlic in 1 tablespoon of oil until lightly colored. In a separate pan, saute zucchini and eggplant. Add tomatoes and seasonings. Combine the first mixture with the eggplant and zucchini. Put the mixture in a pyrex casserole or ovenware. Bake for 15 minutes at 350 degrees in an oven. Serve hot or cold. Serves 4.

THE DINING ROOM

The Ritz-Carlton, Laguna Niguel
33533 Ritz-Carlton Dr.
Dana Point, CA
240-2000

Risotto with Saffron and Truffle

2	cups arborio rice
6	cups white chicken stock
1/2	cup dry white wine
	pinch of saffron
1	truffle with juice
1	cup grated parmesan
5	ounces butter
1	small onion, finely chopped
	salt and pepper to taste

Melt 2 ounces of butter and saute the onion. Add the rice, stir for 2 minutes. Pour in the wine and cook until it evaporates. Add the chicken stock, 2 cups at a time. The rice should always be covered with stock. Add the saffron, minced truffle and the juice from the truffle. When done, add the parmesan, butter and season to taste. Serves six.

RISTORANTE FERRANTELLI
25001 Dana Point Dr.
Dana Point, CA
493-1401

Roasted Peppers

2	*large bell peppers, 1 yellow, 1 red*
4	*teaspoons olive oil*
2	*teaspoons capers*
	salt and pepper to taste
	juice of 1 lemon

Roast peppers on a charbroiler or gas broiler until dark and roasted. Peel and rinse in cold water. Slice and mix with olive oil and capers. Season and add lemon juice. Serves four.

THE OLD DANA POINT CAFE
24720 Del Prado Ave.
Dana Point, CA
661-6003

Greek Scrambled Eggs

12	*beaten eggs*
1	*teaspoon tabasco*
4	*ounces Greek feta cheese*
4	*tablespoons chopped fresh basil leaves*
1	*teaspoon minced garlic*

Beat eggs and fold in the remaining ingredients. In a large pan lightly coated with olive oil, scramble the eggs to desired consistency. Serve with fresh fruit. Serves four.

THE PALM GARDEN

Sheraton Hotel, Newport Beach
4545 MacArthur Blvd.
Newport Beach, CA
833-0570

Mexican and Thai Shrimp Pizza

15   *large shrimp, peeled, veined and cut in half lengthwise*

Thai Shrimp Marinade:

9   *tablespoons olive oil*
5   *tablespoons soy sauce*
2   *tablespoons honey*
3/4   *tablespoon Chinese chili sauce*
       juice of 1 lemon

Combine the marinade ingredients in a bowl and marinate the shrimp for at least 4 hours in the refrigerator.

5   *8 inch flour tortillas*
40   *thin slices roma tomatoes*
1   *bunch chopped cilantro*
1/2   *cup coarsely chopped peanuts*
1   *tablespoon chili flakes*
25   *ounces grated mozzarella cheese*

Brush tortillas with olive oil and lightly grill over mesquite coals until grill marks appear on both sides of the tortillas. Place the tortillas on a baking sheet. Brush each with a little of the shrimp marinade. Sprinkle 5 ounces of cheese on each of the 5 tortillas. Then place 8 slices of tomato on each. Add 6 pieces of shrimp, a pinch of cilantro, a pinch of chili flakes and 1 tablespoon peanuts on each tortilla. Sprinkle on remaining mozzarella. Bake at 450 degrees for 5 minutes or until the cheese is well melted and slightly browned. Serves five.

THE ALLEY

4501 W. Coast Hwy.
Newport Beach, CA
646-9126

The Alley Cat Coffee

1	ounce Myer's rum
1/2	ounce Tia Maria
1/2	ounce Bailey's Irish Cream
	fresh brewed coffee

Combine ingredients in a mug, then add fresh coffee. Top with fresh whipped cream.

MARGARITAVILLE

2332 W. Coast Hwy.
Newport Beach, CA
631-8220

Shark Attack Cocktail

1	ounce Myer's Platinum Rum
3/4	ounce Blue Curacao
1/2	ounce Coco Lopez coconut milk
1/2	ounce orgeat syrup
2	ounces sweet and sour mix

In a blender, put 5 ounces of crushed ice. Combine all ingredients and blend until thoroughly mixed. Pour into a margarita glass. For a special touch, add a shark fin stir stick and add a few drops of red grenadine.

212

BLUE BEET CAFE
107 21st Pl.
Newport Beach, CA
675-2338

Shooting Star

1/2	ounce Smirnoff's Vodka
1/2	ounce Bombay gin
1/2	ounce Bacardi Lite rum
1/4	ounce Hiram Walker Triple Sec
1/4	ounce Amaretto
1 1/2	ounces Coca-Cola
2	ounces sweet and sour mix

Combine all ingredients and chill over ice. Serve in a cocktail glass.

OPASO'S BALBOA THAI CAFE
209 1/2 Palm St.
Balboa, CA
675-0161

Thai Tea

1	cup Thai tea
3/4	cup sugar
1	ounce half and half

Brew 1 cup of Thai tea leaves in a gallon of water for 20 minutes. Drain leaves. Add sugar. Makes 1 gallon. Pour tea over crushed ice. Top with half and half. Optional: Add 1 ounce of 151 rum.

BLUE BEET CAFE

107 21st. Pl.
Newport Beach, CA
675-2338

Tortuga

1/2	ounce Bacardi Lite rum
1/2	ounce Bacardi dark rum
1/2	ounce Myer's rum
1/2	ounce Malibu rum
2	ounces Blue Curacao
	equal parts of orange and pineapple juice

Combine and serve in a Hurricane glass over ice.

DILLMAN'S

801 E. Balboa Blvd.
Balboa, CA
673-7726

Cherry Sauce

3	cups maraschino cherry juice
1	cup dry sherry
1/2	cup brown sugar
1/4	cup concentrated lemon juice
5	ounces Southern Comfort or bourbon
	mixture of cornstarch and water to thicken

Combine all ingredients into a saucepan. Bring to boil and reduce. Add corn starch mixture to thicken to a grabby consistency.

TREES
440 Heliotrope Ave.
Corona del Mar, CA
673-0910

Cilantro-Mint Sauce

1 1/2	bunches fresh cilantro
1/2	bunch fresh parsley
1	bunch fresh mint
1	egg
2	cups peanut oil
1/2	cup plus 2 tablespoons rice vinegar
2	pinches salt
1	pinch white pepper

Carefully wash and drain the herbs (spin dry). Place the egg and vinegar in a blender, cover, turn on to high speed. Remove the cover and with the blender running, drizzle in the oil to emulsify. Add the herbs in 3 portions until they are completely incorporated into the sauce. Season with salt and pepper to taste. Strain through a fine sieve and serve as accompaniment to lamb, fish or chicken.

DILLMAN'S
801 E. Balboa Blvd.
Balboa, CA
673-7726

Mornay Sauce

5	ounces flour
4	ounces onion, finely diced
5	ounces butter
1/2	gallon milk
2	ounces chicken base
1/4	teaspoon white pepper
1/4	teaspoon garlic powder
2	tablespoons non-dairy creamer
3	tablespoons parmesan cheese
2	ounces swiss cheese
1/2	cup white wine

Saute onions in butter until tender. Reduce heat. While constantly stirring, add flour to make a roux. When the roux starts to turn light brown, add milk. On a low heat, add all ingredients except swiss cheese and wine. Cook on low heat for 5 minutes while stirring. Strain the sauce through a China cap. Add swiss cheese and wine.

FIVE CROWNS

3801 E. Coast Hwy.
Corona del Mar, CA
760-0331

Whipped Cream Horseradish Sauce

1/2   pint whipping cream
1/4   cup grated fresh horseradish
1/4   teaspoon Lawry's Seasoned Salt
1/4   teaspoon salt
       dash tabasco sauce

Whip cream until stiff peaks form. Fold in remaining ingredients. Chill 1 hour before using. Yields 2 cups.